THE SCHOOL THEATRE

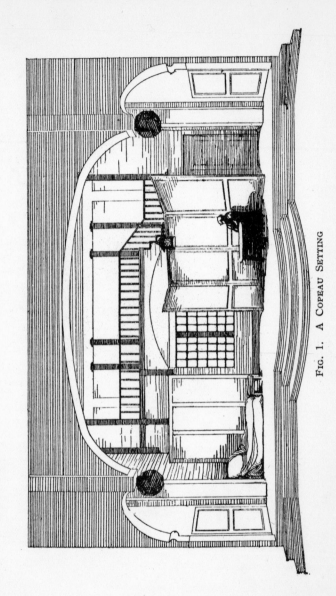

Fig. 1. A Copeau Setting

THE SCHOOL THEATRE

A Handbook of Theory and Practice

BY

ROY MITCHELL

WITH ILLUSTRATIONS BY

JOCELYN TAYLOR

AND INTRODUCTION BY

JOSEPH T. SHIPLEY

NEW YORK
BRENTANO'S
PUBLISHERS

CONTENTS

LIST OF ILLUSTRATIONS

INTRODUCTION

INTRODUCTION

ALMOST a century ago the French playwrights, breaking from the rules of the classicists, inaugurated a period of dramatic experimentation the results of which have surpassed even the enthusiastic dreams of those young Romantics. The early fervor of the group that rallied around Victor Hugo was succeeded by the infinite care and subtle craftsmanship of such technicians as Scribe, Augier, and Sardou. Their work, continued by Pinero and Jones in England, was meanwhile utilized and surpassed in the social dramas of Ibsen. The hostility that met the Norwegian's work a host of staunch supporters overcame; they carried the new technique and spirit of play writing into many fields and fashions. The social comedies of Shaw, the muted mysticism of Maeterlinck: drama is coursing through a period unequalled in rich and varied creations, in ideas and emotions urging to fresh, potent form.

It was inevitable that the craft of the theatre, the arts interwoven in the production of a play, should be enriched from the stimulus of the dramas themselves. The theatre is a game in which competition is cooperation; improvement in any department spurs on the rest. Indeed, the new plays did not merely stimulate, they required, a fresh handling; and the pioneers who were bold enough to produce them were imaginative enough to clothe them in suitable settings and to interpret them with sympathy and insight. As varied as the plays themselves were the styles of presentation. Far from being handicapped by poverty and small quarters, directors evolved out of the very conditions of their production new triumphs of suggestive power. While one dramatic movement, still exemplified in the Moscow Art Players, strove to extend the representative stage to fulness of realistic reproduction, another endeavored to eliminate all appearance of reality, appealing deliberately, as Shakspere did of necessity, to the imagination of the audience. With costumes and delivery attuned to the chosen *décor,* all sought a presentation adapted to the play, individual and harmonious, enforcing and enriching the dramatist's contribution.

This growth from a standardized presentation to a production varying with the play has, of course, been a slow progression; some professional producers still employ an almost fixed form. School productions, unfortunately yet naturally, have almost invariably failed to take advantage of the rich opportunities for vivid, varied conceptions, have continued to employ the stereotyped methods of staging and performance. Countless conflicting tasks besiege the teacher; for him to attend faithfully to his work, to keep abreast of new methods in teaching his subject, and at the same time to follow theatrical progress, would be herculean. Moreover, to schools away from the chief centers of the country's entertainment, the local playhouses may offer little stimulus for experiment and growth—although the many little theatres that have sprung up in the last decade are doing yeoman service for the new stagecraft. Yet even these aspiring groups often need guidance and example; the enthusiastic activity of thousands of young men and women, of thousands of high school youths and elementary school children, is at the beck of directors with faith in the value of their work, with love of human relationships and of the theatre, with sympathetic understanding of the problems of the craft.

In the present volume, Mr. Roy Mitchell presents to such persons the basic theory and sound practical advice which they must have. Avoiding the failures and the excesses of recent experimentation, he has garnered the fruit of the new growth, with sensitive discrimination and with intimate understanding of the problems of the school group or the club. He accepts the inevitable limitations of small stage and ill-equipped auditorium, and suggests how these may be overcome, may be shaped to added power.

The three types of scenery Mr. Mitchell discusses— the draped stage, the cyclorama-representative stage, and the Copeau stage—are those most frequently used in professional performances, and one of them should, whenever possible, be developed as part of a permanent equipment. For an unpretentious beginning, however, or for whimsies or plays with younger children, a setting devised by Moritz Jagendorf for The Children's Playhouse may be effectively employed. This consists merely of several large frames—three are enough—each made in two hinged sections five feet high and two feet wide;

slipped into or tacked onto these frames are panels of cardboard painted to suggest the scene or the mood.* The cardboard may be painted on both sides, so that "a turn is a change," or other strips may be ready for new scenes. Place one or two of these in the center rear, and one on either side of the stage; they will create the desired atmosphere. Dressing the scene-shifters as pages renders a front curtain unnecessary, though with these panel settings a loosely draped rear curtain will help neutralize the background and leave the fancy free to follow the mood of the acting.

Fully as important as the changes in style of scenery are the recent developments in stage lighting. Devices have been invented of such adaptability and power that in certain novel productions the light itself has been the scenery; and no one can foretell to what extent the Clavilux, or color-organ, will replace the curtain drop. Lighting is already, perhaps, the chief element in staging. In the production of Kaiser's "From Morn to Midnight," for example, a tree that in the refugee's fancy turns to a ghost is easily transformed by using instead of painted scenery two slides, one with the gaunt winter tree, one with the skeleton, and slipping these in front of the light that floods the white canvas above the snowy ground. But even when employed simply as an aid in suggesting the tone of the play, or as a purely mechanical expedient for centering attention on a character or a portion of the

* For a detailed description of these frames, and a simple method of construction, consult the preface to "One-Act Plays for Young Folks," edited by M. A. Jagendorf, Brentano's.

stage, lighting his been so improved and so simplified that the best equipment is not beyond the reach of the humblest organization. Very recently some successful efforts to shadow projection have revealed another angle of light-usefulness. In Dan Totheroh's prize play, "Wild Birds," the two little runaways listen, in front of a large tent, to the cries of a revivalist preacher and the groans of his "mourners," whose shadows, cast from behind upon the canvas, loom threateningly upon the apprehensive pair. In Pierre Loving's "The Stick-Up" an opposite arrangement proves even more suggestive; crouched behind a box or standing in a pit at the front of the stage, three invisible figures cast eerie shadows upon the vault of the sky—the curving back of the stage—as in their dream the highwaymen prepare to "hold up" a comet. For mysterious or fantastic presentations, such as these, the device of the shadowgraph holds forth rich promise; for every possible requirement of the director or limitation of the particular theatre a suitable lighting effect may be devised.

While Mr. Mitchell presents a long and varied list of plays for the new stagecraft, with many old favorites of the little theatre and many newer intriguing pieces, the creative talent latent in any working group should be encouraged. Stimulated by one or two successful productions of selected plays, by the activity of scene-designer, scene-builder, costumer, director, and stage-manager, some members will feel the urge to write something for his fellow-workers to produce. Even though the resultant piece will almost inevitably fall short of much that might be chosen, the present writer has found that the occasional production of a play rising out of the enthusiasm of an active group is amply rewarded in increased zeal and fired imagination. If workers so imbued be guided by one equipped with insight and with an understanding of the theatre, the club, the school, the community, cannot but be enriched. And anyone who has struggled through a long apprenticeship to a vantage-point in school or club production, must often have wished for an approach so clear and so stimulating as Mr. Mitchell's, to the fundamental principles and rules of practice of the modern theatre.

JOSEPH T. SHIPLEY

New York
1925

I. THE RETURN OF THE THEATRE

IN A little book like this, where my first object is to offer practical hints to school theatre workers, I can spare little space towards the persuasion of those not already converted, to the growing practice of presenting drama in our schools. The rising tide of a movement throughout the English speaking world will satisfy them by its volume and its results far better than I can by my arguments, that the association of school with theatre giving the former new zest and the latter new cultural impulses is destined to liberate great forces for coming generations.

We say of our schools that they conserve culture. But there are kinds of culture that are not readily conserved by our present teaching processes. They cannot be communicated; they must be elicited by other means than we have so far possessed. This is true most of the interpretative and fine arts. No lecture can transmit their magic. They must be taught by some kind of apprenticeship. Song is learned by delight in singing, and painting by absorption in the mystery of delineation and colour.

Our desires lead us. They quicken mind until mind rises and puts them aside because they interfere with its new quickness. A child or a man will look dully upon the best painting in the world until desire provokes in him the will to do something like it. Finely spoken English will leave him cold until he has desired to utter fine English; poetry will be a tasteless thing until poetry touches his life, and sculpture an indifferent kind of

9

bric-a-brac until there has been created in him an urgent need to know the laws that lie behind it.

How shall we quicken his desire? We have no need to urge him to know about gas engines. Every boy is an automotive engineer because motors touch intimately his desire to travel sixty miles an hour. What means can we find, then, to stir his desire to know the arts? Where can we make them touch his life? Educationists believe now, and they are justifying their belief, that the living link with a creative feeling for the arts is in the school theatre.

This, of course, is not our first commerce with the theatre as a means to education. We have done many school plays in years past, but until a very few years ago we thought the theatre was entirely a matter of actors, and if we spoke of it as having a cultural value we regarded that value as having to do with declamation and posturing. And as we saw it, so we imitated it, mostly, I think, to our discredit. Certainly nobody took us very seriously. Since then, however, we have found that the theatre is far more a place of visible beauty than we ever supposed, that it is foster-parent of a hundred beautiful crafts and of manifold disciplines that can all serve the enrichment of life.

I am not sure at just what point we forgot it. The Greeks certainly knew it and made a great and heartening culture around it. I think that perhaps the Romans lost it. Their instinct was to hire their actors and so the art failed them as athletics fail us when we are content to do nothing more than watch professional athletes.

Now that we are bringing the theatre home again among our own people, not the old theatre of prodigies and courtezans and a race apart, but the older theatre of people who serve it because they love it, we can make it live in the measure that we conceive it in its entirety and learn to look upon it seriously as a potent servant of life.

We must not regard it merely as a pastime. We may call it recreation if we like, and if we use the word in its fine sense. We must regard it indeed as a creative and meliorating force in the community, as giving the widest play to the artistic faculties of its people, as being a point of departure for all the arts and a bond between them, and as enriching life for both worker and beholder.

The present opportunity is with the schools. They are the custodians of our ideals as a people, and the generation that can do most to bring the wealth of the theatre back into our life is now in their keeping. For the teacher who has seen the possibilities of the theatre as an aid to the school, who has seen that an apprenticeship to any of its branches can help the pupil, can give him creative and interpretative courage, can develop his sense of cooperation and his ability to subordinate himself to a common end; for the teacher who has the imagination to perceive how much a generation so trained can give to the life of its town and country, these notes have been made.

They are only notes, chosen to afford the greatest possible aid in the difficulties the director of a school theatre must encounter. I have tried to include as many as space will allow of the things he is unlikely to find in other books. Throughout I speak of the director as summing up the activity, and I assume that a director, actual or potential is my reader, because, after all, however many persons share in it, a theatre revolves around the enthusiasm of one man or woman. Moreover, although I say "school" throughout, most of the book is primarily of the theatre and the suggestions it contains will serve for any group whether of a school or not.

Perhaps in most things I am aiming too high, and urge too much. I leave it for my reader to modify as he goes.

II. DEFINING THE AIM

THE first essential to success in a school theatre is a clear idea of the manner in which the work is to be carried on. This would seem so obvious as to be scarcely worth saying but there are many possible formations in non-professional playmaking and the reader will do well to study them carefully until he has satisfied himself, first, that what he proposes to do exactly fits his needs, second, that it permits of such expansion as may be required of him, and third, that his undertaking is not too ambitious to be maintained steadily and rhythmically as a permanent activity.

Of course if there is no greater purpose than to make one play for a special occasion, and perhaps another a year or so later, it will not matter much how the production is conceived. Such an adventure has little to recommend it either educationally or artistically and can be done in almost any way. The director must bear his headache like a man and heal the inevitable quarrels as best he may.

If, however, he is convinced that such a work has to be carried on regularly and that it is better to do several small productions at definite intervals than one big one, he has certain questions to answer and certain requirements to fulfill.

His first questions will be: "What is the form of the group making the plays? In what manner is it to proceed, and in what relation to what audience? Whence does it derive its revenue and what revenue can it expect? Is it to exist primarily for class work by pupils and for pupils?

If it is to be a direct application of the dramatic method to the study of literature, having no more contact with the outside world of parents and friends than is required for a concert or for closing exercises, it can proceed very simply indeed, and the more simply the better. It will need no money beyond a small sum for initial equipment. A few draperies for background and to screen the usual entrances, a curtain—or preferably no curtain—will be enough. The other accessories can be borrowed or improvised, or can be made up in a few hours and used many times. In such an activity staging should be reduced to the bare minimum and the entire focus of the work should be centred in the acting. In such a formation everybody can have his chance to act, everybody will receive his training in reading and stage movement. This is an excellent formation, and will serve the needs of many schools either permanently or as a step to something wider. The director should ponder well whether he will stay in this field, use it as a step to a larger one, or, passing it altogether, begin with a wider purpose. If he decides to do the last, certain drastic revisions of organization are necessary.

In this case he asks himself: Is the theatre to exist for the pupils, their relatives and their friends? Are the performances to be given by the pupils for an outside audience? Is its revenue to be derived from paid admissions? In such case the formation will have to be much more like that of a professional theatre. The director will have to select his actors more carefully and use the best of them more frequently. It does not do to ask people to pay to see an inept actor playing a part because it is his turn. He must only play it because within the limits of the company it is his part. Such a requirement makes it inevitable that many pupils will be debarred from acting altogether. This is no hardship so long as acting is not the only thing the group does. Therefore, in order to keep the non-actors and their friends from demanding a rotation of parts the director must emphasize the crafts end of the work. He may, for a time, be able to ignore this necessity and evade the demand for parts, but in a few months he will be reduced to his sediment of incompetents and the venture cannot live. This is the ailment that carries off nine out of ten amateur societies.

It is when the director adopts a better scenic method that the greatest value enters into school playing, and in this formation the fullest opportunity is afforded for work in the plastic and decorative arts. This is also the point at which non-professional playing can be raised into a fine art or can be allowed to degenerate into mere indulgence.

Here is the issue of which I have spoken, and unless the director understands it he is fated to indifferent success, or probably to complete failure. In his preoccupation with results the layman is prone to neglect causes in the theatre and to forget that every professional play he sees is the product of sixty or seventy persons working all or part of their time on it. The extent to which specialization is carried in the trades of the theatre makes this an unduly large number. None the less it is an index of what is required for good work. In the little theatres the number is greatly reduced but the best establishments allow for a proportion of two executives or craftsmen for each actor. The work can be done with half as many non-actors but directors soon find good reasons why it should not.

If therefore the director has satisfied himself that his task is to make successive productions—in whatever style—for a related but outside public, and if he expects to carry on his work by means of revenue so derived, he must organize three corps, one to act, one to make the production and tend stage, and a third to look after the front of the house. His acting corps should be used as a company is used, over and over again with an effort to train likely candidates for it, but with as little concession to the "rotation of parts" theory as will serve to keep the peace. The technical staff must be given every possible credit for work done and must be made to feel the dignity and importance of their part of the production.

There remains a third formation in which the work can be carried on, one suited to smaller communities where the school is the natural centre for recreational activities and where it is desirable to extend the work to a wider field than among the pupils themselves. This is a formation which the director should examine carefully because he may find himself forced into it as his work expands and he will save some heartburning if he provides for it at the start. Is it to be a play-making activity which, using the school for its centre and availing itself of the school's facilities, will make plays by pupils and others for the entire community?

There are great advantages here, and, if the conditions permit, it is the ideal arrangement. It provides a living link between the school and its public, it gives the school more direct access to the cultural activities of the town, it opens a way for a host of other activities and provides a wide and healthy means of recreation for many persons. It puts the whole establishment on a firmer footing. In such case, of course, the pupils themselves contribute less to the acting but they do more in the actual making and handling of the production, and they have the added distinction of working on an even footing with their seniors each in his own department of the work.

Most important of all, this third formation gives a wider variety of actors and permits the use of grown-ups for older parts, thus giving an opportunity for presenting much more acceptable plays and ensuring a far greater revenue. Even if a director cannot see his way to it at first he should provide for the necessity of drawing upon outsiders to fill difficult parts. The pupils should be taught, and this is one of the means to it, that a good performance is more important than any individual's pleasure. It does them no harm to find out that their plays exist not for themselves alone but for their town as well and that they as participants must serve a wider interest than to flaunt themselves. There are always a few young egoists who will gather in corners and argue that their play exists for their gratification. For a time they will make trouble but they will soon learn that every theatre exists for the gratification of the audience or it ceases to exist at all for lack of an audience. The theatre affords a great discipline in hospitality.

If the director determines to proceed along the lines I have first described (as of pupils for pupils) he will require only a simple organization. His whole group will be of players with the addition of a stage manager to keep order in the entrances, a mechanician to set his drapery apparatus, a property master and probably a wardrobe directress to take care of whatever cloaks and other garments he needs.

If he decides upon either of the other two courses he will need a larger staff. He will require first of all an assistant to relieve him of some of the detail that makes play production so trying. He will need also four chiefs of departments, first, a regisseur of company, second, a stage manager, third, a house manager, and fourth, a musical director. I am not inventing jobs. These are essential executives and without them he can get into serious difficulties.

Regisseur of company used to be called in English theatres chief prompter, but this name is falling into disuse because he does not prompt any more. He has an assistant who does that. His are other and more exacting duties, especially in a non-professional group. He calls rehearsals, makes the playing script as rehearsals proceed, allots dressing space, gives out costumes, calls time—half-hour, fifteen minutes, overture, first act, and so on—is responsible for offstage cues, appoints prompters, dressers, and makes any protests on behalf of his corps as against any other department. He is the steward of a liner, the manager of a big hotel, a diplomat and a martinet. A group with a good regisseur of company rides on air.

The stage manager controls everything else behind scenes. He rings up and down, he supervises the handling of everything, directs changes of scene, and maintains quiet in the wings.

The house manager is responsible for everything before the curtain, and for all links with the public. He is the theatre's official host.

The musical director's duties need no description.

The regisseur's staff consists of the prompter proper, the wardrobe directress and any other persons whom he requires from time to time.

The stage manager's staff consists of three chiefs, each with his crew. The first is the chief mechanician, who has charge of the carpenter shop and the handling of all scenery on the stage. The second is the property master who has charge of furniture, carpets, pictures, curtains, flowers, weapons and hand properties. His crew sweep up, buy small articles and make whatever properties have to be made. The electrician has charge of all illuminants and whatever water-service may be required.

The house manager's staff—treasurer, doorman, ushers, publicity man—need no description.

The foregoing are all executives of performance. The director may add as he requires, or as persons offer themselves, production assistants whose activities are confined to the workshop and cease when rehearsals are over, such as, an art director who designs scenes, a dress designer, a scene painter, dress-makers, property workers in papier mâché, leather, wood, plaster or metal. These are at his discretion and perhaps as happens in the biggest theatres, two or three people will fulfill all the duties. They should if possible be kept to such work, duly credited with it, and relieved of all other duties. They with the four chiefs will probably prove to be the real heart of the theatre and the enduring element in it.

The list I have given may seem complicated and even unnecessary but the filling of these essential posts is the first step towards efficiency and a pleasant life. A single play can be given with one or two frenzied pack-horses doing everything, but sustained work requires a strict distribution of responsibility. The professional worker in the theatre knows this and until the amateur finds it out he will always be clumsy and ridiculous. Not only does such distribution of work give facility but it gives dignity to the non-actor who has too long been considered an amiable servant   An efficient staff is a great check on the uncertain temperament of actors, and its very size strengthens the director's hand. These technicians want a good show and they will be detached enough to see that nothing petty prevents them from getting it. They will ensure discipline where the director cannot.

In the best permanent theatres the focus of consciousness is in the executive and technical staffs, and this is doubly desirable in a non-professional group. The actor then becomes a guest to be treated hospitably, and given every consideration. When an amateur technician makes a mistake it does not do to reprimand him as one might a hired stage hand. He will merely quit. One can say to him however, "We are not giving So-and-So a chance. We are failing in our capacity of hosts," and the reproof is fair. The actors get their reward in applause. They are taken out to supper. The poor crew when the show is over have nothing to do but wipe their faces with a piece of waste and go home to bed. The wise director who values the morale of his theatre pitches in his lot with the crew.

III. ADAPTATION TO CONDITIONS

HAVING settled on his manner of playing and his organization, the next responsibility of the director of a school theatre is to determine his technical method. It will be well for him to make at the start a careful survey of his limitations and also of his resources These are the things that will dictate his technique. Too often a school director chooses a method merely because he wants it, irrespective of what facilities he has for it. Then after one desperate effort to carry out his plan, he gives up.

His first task is to adapt his whole work to the room or hall in which he must play, making the most of its peculiarities and creating a style of presentation based on existing conditions. If he does this well and courageously he can achieve a distinction that mere expenditure cannot give him. He must in effect evolve his own kind of theatre. The greatest handicap to directness and sincerity in adapted halls is the clutter of poor imitations of things that belong to the standard theatre. At a time when the best artists of the theatre are striving to get away from the Italian opera stage there is something pathetic in the effort of community producers to torture curtains and drapes into a weak semblance of what the advanced theatre is trying to eliminate.

If the director will always keep in mind that the essential art of the theatre is of a human body in motion, and words spoken to explain and amplify that motion, he will have learned the most important truth he can know. Everything beyond that simple requirement is a luxury that can easily become a vanity unless it is kept in proper proportion to the necessities of movement.

A raised platform is not essential. It is only desirable. Desirable also is a door at each side of the scene by which actors may enter or leave. A minimum of twenty feet of width of playing floor is almost essential because of the thickness of the actor's body and the fact that bodies obscure each other on a narrower stage as soon as the actors are grouped in different planes. Wide wing-space at the sides is not essential except to a clumsy stage-manager who does not know how to pack his stuff. Height of opening is not so important as is often supposed; twelve feet from the floor is plenty for all ordinary purposes. Footlights are not essential, and unless used with great skill they are execrable. Neither is spaciousness of auditorium of great moment. Amateur performances cost nothing to repeat, and repetition is good for both actors and staff. It is better far to do three performances for a hundred people each time, than one lone performance for three hundred. It is better to make sure of plenty of room for each person and good aisle space than to feel that some advantage is to be gained by crowding in a big audience.

The director should assume as basic in his theatre any outstanding characteristics of the hall whether it conforms to standard theatre usage or not. He should not use it apologetically but should make a distinction out of his necessity. If he has a pillar awkwardly placed on his stage, or an inconvenient flight of stairs, or a jog in a wall, he should take that feature for granted and play around it, converting it or disguising it each time into an element suited to his needs. He will get a vigour and freshness into his work, which he could never

get otherwise.   A good designer of scene will actually
go out of his way to get what the amateur designer
laments.   He will put a paper weight down somewhere
in his stage plan and design around it, making all his
scenes clear of the obstacle.   This, he finds, gives him
fertility as well as harmony in his settings.

These are general suggestions and in my present
space, I cannot deal with all the problems which the
conversion of a hall must create.   The following advice to the director will meet a few of the commoner
contingencies:

Dismiss all ideas of our existing theatre as an object
for imitation.   Inadequate copies only breed unpleasant
comparisons.   The franker the method the more it
disarms criticism.   Stand at the back of the hall and try
to see a method.   Do not think of a theatre stage at all.
Think of actors moving and of what decorative elements
would be needed to give conviction to their motion.
See a play in progress, a love scene, a procession entering.
Where could comedians sit?   Where would a fight look
most real?   Where would it create the greatest suspense?
Where would it have the greatest comic value?   Doing
this you will find that the motion will create the form of
the theatre.

Deal broadly with every problem.   If the dressing
rooms are at the wrong end of the hall let the actors go
down the aisle to the stage.   Any conformity to need is
good art.   It is only bad art when it is an affectation.

Do not deprive yourself of more important things to
buy a front curtain.   The guillotine drop curtain as
well as the draw curtain are now on trial in the theatre
and may be convicted any day of having done more
harm than good.   They develop hole-and-corner methods

and petty efforts after illusion. If your draperies are few, hang them behind actors instead of in front of scene shifters. Without a curtain you will be spared many scenic vanities. What changes you must make can be made in the dark. The snap of an electric switch will end an act far better than a curtain that only works every other time it is drawn and gets a laugh every time.

Avoid a high stage. Table height is plenty in a moderately large hall. Never let anybody build you a raked or sloping stage. It is the survival of a silly whim of *ballerinas*.

So much for the adaptation of technique to hall. The scenic method must be based on such technique as is required, and upon the general policy of the group. The development of the new stagecraft provides several scenic methods. From these I select three as suited to the various needs described. The first is the use of a set of conventional draperies. The second is the use of a cyclorama sky-cloth and representative scene elements. The third is what is called the Copeau stage, by far the most beautiful and plastic conventional method that has yet come out of the new movement in the theatre.

Draperies need present little trouble and can be dealt with briefly. They will do in any room, with or without a platform and may be affixed directly to the walls or, better, on a pipe-batten so placed that it permits passage behind and on both sides of the stage. The best form of batten is a modified half circle—three sides of a rectangle with rounded corners—made of half-inch pipe jointed in such a way as to make it easily removable. Figure 2 shows a good model. If there is a ceiling beam anywhere near the edge of the stage the draperies should come forward to it. The beam will be useful for masking overhead lamps. The best fabric is a coarse natural coloured linen hung in single strips. Each strip has a liberal hem above as a sleeve through which the pipe may

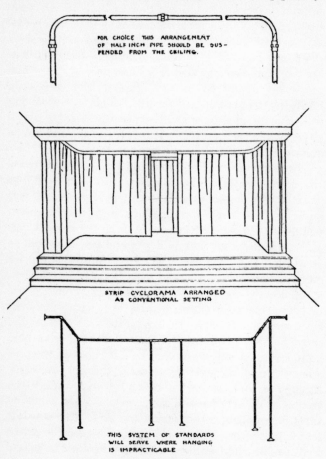

FOR CHOICE THIS ARRANGEMENT
OF HALF INCH PIPE SHOULD BE SUS-
PENDED FROM THE CEILING.

STRIP CYCLORAMA ARRANGED
AS CONVENTIONAL SETTING

THIS SYSTEM OF STANDARDS
WILL SERVE WHERE HANGING
IS IMPRACTICABLE

FIG. 2. A CYCLORAMA DRAPERY

pass, and a hem below to carry sand or shot bags or any kind of metal slugs for weights. A full set of curtains should cover the pipe and provide half as much again for fullness. The fabric hanging thus in folds will not gape between strips. To get a door opening it is only necessary to push back the cloth at the desired place. Windows may be painted on pieces of canvas and pinned to the fabric, as also may friezes or other decorations. The properties should be of the simplest sort, necessary furniture, trees in tubs and the like. This type of setting will serve for all purposes and is epecially suited to plays, given by pupils for pupils. It is easy to hang and can be and should be used without a front curtain.

The same piece of equipment is the first requisite for the second-method—the representative one—and the director who desires to start with a purely conventional outfit and to develop gradually into pictorial scenery, will do well to get a cyclorama of as large size as he can accommodate in his hall, in depth and height as well as in width. For class use it will serve him for a draped stage and when he wishes to make a bigger production it will become his sky-cloth, that cloak which covers our multitude of sins on the stage, and is the basis of modern stage setting. It hangs in place all the time whether the scene be interior or exterior, and if flooded with blue light serves as sky wherever sky can be seen whether among trees, through a window, through an arch, through a door, or past a corner of wall. When the setting is an exterior the scene elements are solids or three dimensional pieces set on the stage just as furniture is in a room. When a cyclorama is used the entire scene can be made with one element, a fountain, a hedge, a statue, a tree-trunk, a pylon, a jut of wall and a balus-

trade, or two or three pillars There is no masking or
tricking of planes or scheming one bit of foliage to go
behind another to screen the back wall of the stage. The
actors can come into the scenes around the ends or can
slip through the folds at the sides. There are no fly-
borders and no clumsy top-hamper to get fouled. A
pillar or any high piece continues to the ceiling. The
good modern showman stands as much and hangs as
little of his scenery as he can.

The pictorial method applied to interior settings is no
more complicated but is a little more expensive, and a
wise director possessed of a cyclorama and starting out
to acquire scenery will be well advised to begin with
plays needing only an exterior of rather fanciful spirit,
and then collect his interior elements bit by bit in the
form of pilasters, pillar-pieces and sections of exterior
wall. If he proceed thus along a well arranged plan he
will find himself at the end of a year or so with enough
flats for any kind of interior setting. The desideratum
for the greatest possible range of use is about sixteen
elements, the construction and handling of which I shall
describe in the next section.

There remains to be described the Copeau conventional method of staging with some of its applications as
well as the modifications possible for school use. M.
Jacques Copeau at his Theatre du Vieux-Colombier in
Paris has developed and applied to modern use a Shakes-
pearean stage with front, rear and upper playing areas.
Fig. 1 shows it set for performance. Figure 4 shows the
skeleton elements employed in it. For this method he
requires nothing but a rectangular hall, one end of which
has two doors at right and left of the stage These doors
should lead into corridors, or flanking rooms which can

be used for dressing or wing space. The doors are the normal and visible entrance to the stage. More of them are an advantage but only the two mentioned are essential Copeau's stage is low and at the Vieux-Colombier is actually made of concrete. The front line of the stage could be straight but in order to break the sharp division between actor and audience and to get fluency instead, he carries it forward at sides and centre, allowing it to flow to the floor in a series of steps. The second essential in a Copeau stage is the upper screen or canopy. Decoratively it bounds the top of the screen, practically it conceals the lighting apparatus. It is a light framework treated architecturally and in most halls should be removable in three or four pieces. The third requisite is a device for giving an upper or mezzanine playing floor. Copeau made several experiments in his search for the simplest and most convenient mezzanine. The principle of the early ones is shown in Figure 3. Finally under the supervision of Louis Jouvet, who is Copeau's designer and technician as well as his most skilful actor, there was evolved the set of elements shown in Figure 4. They are of skeleton construction, capable of being folded up when not in use and may be moved to any position on stage. They are characterless as they stand and form the armature on which is fastened whatever scenery the play requires.

Copeau's practice with this triple stage is to set the whole of it at once, and, using no front curtain or act-drop, to leave it set throughout the performance, moving his action from one part of it to another. If he requires a house interior he will set a big room with a lower floor, stairs, and an upper hall or balcony. If it is to be the garden in front of a house, he will dress the mezzanine

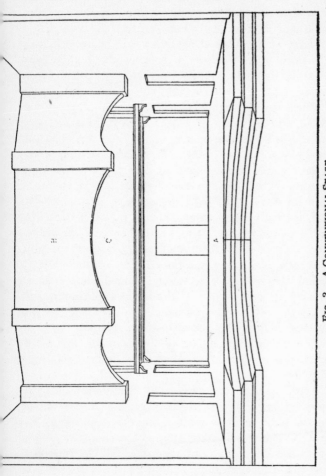

FIG. 3. A CONVENTIONAL STAGE

THE ELEMENTS SHOWN ABOVE CONSIST OF (A) THE PLATFORM (B) THE CANOPY TO CONCEAL THE LIGHTING AND (C) A MEZZANINE WHICH CREATES AN UPPER AND AN INNER PLAYING AREA FOR ELIZABETHAN AND FOR MODERN USE.

front to serve as a house, and make the main lower stage his garden. Under the mezzanine he may have a room which can be revealed when needed. He may set a cliff-edge with a ledge above and a cave below. It may be a street with windows or balcony above and doors below and the main stage becomes the road itself. There is scarcely any limit to its mutability.

When the spectators enter the hall, the stage, dimly lighted, is in full view. The decoration of the scene may stop at the stage line or may run a little way into the house along the side walls. There is no cutting off at the proscenium line as in our modern theatre. Perhaps the scene is the house interior I spoke of. In this case the main stage is the big living-room or drawing-room, furnished with piano, lamps, chairs, tables, settees. A stair leads to the gallery which is the library of the house. There may be doors leading off at the sides of it and a balustrade along the spectator's side of the gallery. Behind the gallery is a stately stained-glass window towering up to the roof. Under the mezzanine, when in the course of the action portieres are drawn back, is the entrance hall of the house, a little reception room in which a whole scene might be played on the arrival or departure of a guest. It is cut off with the portieres when not in use.

A bell sounds, the auditorium light fades, a light comes up on some part of the stage, a character enters and the play begins. Perhaps the first scene is in the library above. When it is finished the characters move to the head of the stairs and stand there talking. As they do so a light picks them up and the library light may dim a little, unless a character with a scene to come in a moment remains there. Then, possibly, the action goes

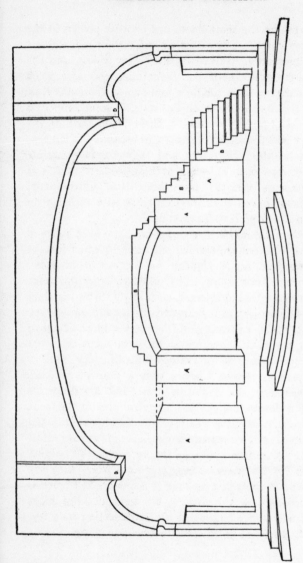

FIG. 4. ELEMENTS OF A COPEAU STAGE

THIS IS THE MOST PLASTIC OF ALL CONVENTIONAL STAGES. BY THE USE OF MOVEABLE PIECES IT ESCAPES ANY OF THE FIXITY OF THE GALLERY IN FIG. 3. THE ELEMENTS A.A.A.A. ARE MADE IN FRAME-WORK TO FOLD UP WHEN NOT IN USE. THE PIECES B.B. ARE MADE RIGID. A PLATFORM PIECE CAN BE USED IF IT IS NECESSARY TO CROSS AT C. AT THE VIEUX-COLOMBIER LAMPS TO LIGHT THE ACTORS ARE HUNG AT D.D. FIG. 1 IS APPROX-IMATELY THIS ARRANGEMENT WITH SCENERY IN PLACE.

to a settee on the main floor, and another person in the play may enter. The actors sit and talk or move about in this new area. Presently the visitor leaves, and the play moves up to the door. Sometimes a scene is taken between an actor on the floor and one on the gallery, or one on the floor and one on the stair, or sometimes in a little nook beside the stair. There is no part of the scene to which the actors cannot go because the stage is as wide as the auditorium and they are fully visible wherever they are. There is nothing to drive them out into tiresome straight lines and little unsupported groupings in a well-worn stage centre as actors are forced to stand in our picture-frame stage.

All the false and tricky things we have ever believed our theatre to be, are washed out in one blessed instant when we first see a Copeau production in progress. This is the actor's home. The ample and spacious stage with its many foci of interest, each in its turn picked up in high light-colour as it is needed and let slip away when it is not, make a dream world out of the most literal of modern necessities, and never for a moment does the convention violate the spectator's sense of unity.

Sometimes indeed Copeau uses a pair of traverse curtains—never the guillotine drop—but his draperies are only a device to give him a neutral area at the front of the stage, or to close off the rear half of his scene when he wishes to set a screen and a few pieces of furniture that will suggest another house, an inn, or some other setting required for his play. These curtains, when they are used, hang in folds just upstage of the doors in Figure 4. This, however, is a luxury of his method. For most plays it will suffice to suggest the extra setting by a few elements disclosed in the under-mezzanine space.

In Twelfth Night the main stage floor is the garden with garden-seats and clipped trees in boxes. The gallery is Olivia's terrace, reached by a broad stair, or through tall Italian windows at the back of the mezzanine. The under-space is screened by glazed windows and when these are thrown open it becomes a room in the house for comedians. When the traverse curtains are closed the front of the stage represents the coast of Illyria.

It is unbelievably simple and plastic. While it provides every opportunity for ingenious arrangement and fine decoration, it can be used so economically as to require only a few dollars for production. There is no effort after illusion, nothing to conceal. The stage provides director and actor with every advantage of differences of level, of interrelation and of spacing that the heart can desire. Most of all it creates atmosphere and arouses the imagination of the audience, a great thing in these days when we think it is the function of the art of the theatre to challenge our audience with realistic scenery and demand that they say where we have failed to imitate nature. An audience antagonized thus at the start will remain antagonistic throughout the evening. An audience whose imagination is aroused will continue to use imagination all through the play.

For the conversion of old churches, old halls and big rooms the Copeau method cannot be surpassed. It requires no wing room and costs little to install. For new halls where it is intended that plays will be given the method is ideal and architects should be persuaded to take advantage of it. It only requires the spacing of already necessary doors, and a fixed or removable screen which is in itself an attractive feature in a big room.

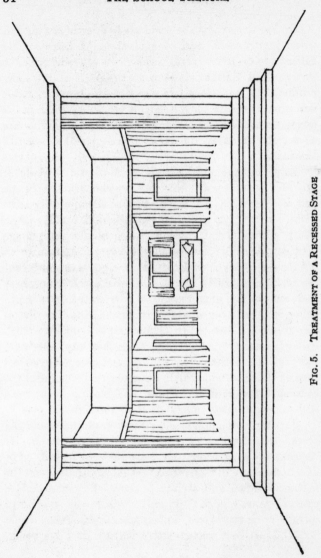

FIG. 5.   TREATMENT OF A RECESSED STAGE

The screen can be made to carry every bit of the lighting equipment and the walls can be kept clear of unsightly lamps and wiring. A convenient treatment of such a room would be that shown in Figure 3 with whatever railing to the gallery the decoration of the room might require. The movable mezzanine elements are very simple and can be made to pack away when not wanted. If it is thought desirable to make scenic productions in the modern manner, the canopy device gives ample top masking and a traverse curtain can be run along behind it. Top masking is always the great problem of the non-professional director.

It is not only in the hope that many schools and community groups will provide themselves with the Copeau elements that I have described the technique at so great length, but because there is contained in Copeau's method a clue to the spirit in which non-professional playing should be carried on. Even if such an equipment is beyond the means of a pioneer in any community he will find in the principles underlying it a solution to most of his problems. If he cannot contrive the mezzanine and the canopy he can still, in most halls, employ the forward-and-back technique, using his forestage as a neutral area that will derive its character from whatever scene elements he places on his back stage.

Figure 5 shows an adaptation of this forward-and-back method for one of those little hole-in-the-wall stages which architects love so dearly. They are poky little rooms with openings like a postage stamp in a great expanse of end wall. They are usually flanked by two equally poky dressing rooms borrowed from the space that should have been given to the stage. The stages consequently are never wide enough, never high enough from floor to ceiling and are nearly always too deep. They are reached through side doors by a flight of three criminal steps. With such an arrangement thrust upon him the director should throw a forestage across his entire room and use the recess only as Copeau uses the under-mezzanine area. He will assume then that his forestage is the stage proper and that the picture elements in his recess are only for the purpose of giving his play period and character. If the recess has a curtain it can be drawn while scene elements are being changed. The rear stage should never be more than a symbol of something and no effort should be made to keep the action inside it. When the rear stage is a room, the entire stage is that same room. When the recess shows a house front, the whole stage is a street. The hangings behind the forestage and at the sides should run from the sides of the recess right around to the front of the forestage. At the meeting of stage front and wall the director should hang a big piece of sacking shaped to represent a pilaster. This will shelter lamps or a prompter.

The same process should be followed with that rather more possible but extremely trying type of stage with a big arched proscenium and a cramped depression behind it like the inside of a sea-shell. The stage floor is usually much too high, as well as much too slippery, and the footlights never light more than the actor's feet. The director should work his people on a forestage right across the room if possible and use the sea-shell chiefly for the scene elements that will give character to his play. If the picture space is at all large the scene pieces should be made big enough to fill it to the top.

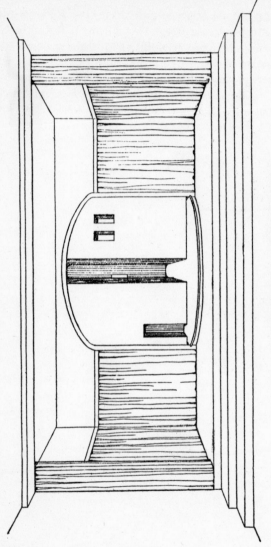

FIG. 6. TREATMENT OF A SHALLOW STAGE

(Figure 6).   In this way the director can get some beautiful effects at little cost.

Every other problem will yield to similar treatment. The secret of conversion of unsuitable halls is to use the greatest possible width and height available, and to try to create the impression that the entire auditorium is the place in which the scene is supposed to be.

IV. SCENE BUILDING AND PAINTING

IN SCENIC work of a pictorial nature the director should be bound by the most important rule of modern stagecraft: Never attempt to show more of anything than in life would actually go on the stage, and preferably, show less. For example on a stage eighteen feet wide and ten feet deep he should not try to set three walls of a living-room, returning two to the proscenium at both sides. He should set only one or at most two walls and let his room run off at the side as if it finished somewhere outside the stage opening. Or he should set a door and a piece of wall, or two pieces of wall and a big casement window between, or an arch leading into another room, a window, a window-seat and a fireplace, making them actually larger than they would be in life. The rest of the room can always be assumed. When he gets one of those playbooks with a neat quadrilateral showing a room that never was on sea or land, with all the furniture pencilled in by the author, he should follow the practice of good directors and tear that page deftly out of the book.

The rule about size applies even more to exteriors than to interiors. If the directions say: "A city square" he should set only one convincing element of a city square, a bit of masonry at the base of a statue, and the feet only of the figure above, or a portico or a doorway. If it is a place in the forest he should set only one massive tree trunk and perhaps a bit of two other trunks at the sides. If he requires a terrace he can get it with a big pillar and a few feet of massive balustrade, masking the sides with hanging clumps of green sacking that might

39

be cypress trees or anything. The audience will forget them in a moment. Golovine used to hang tapestry pieces at the sides of his scenes just to remind people that they were in a theatre.

The scale of everything on a stage must be magnified, *never diminished*. The actor always looks bigger because he is nearer the spectator and because he is above the eye level. Doors should be higher, windows should be bigger and deeper, and stairs should be wider. A throne must be a big throne, a candelabrum must be a tall candelabrum, and so on. Spears on a stage are not fencers' weapons, but are essence of spears and must be tall and stately, or they will be merely silly. A stage opening in the new theatre is a window shoved up against all the world and the most important thing about a scene is that it shall create a world that stretches past both sides of the proscenium frame.

Scene-making is a very easy craft so far as its processes are concerned and most of the mistakes that get amateurs into trouble are easily mended, if the amateur will use his eyes. Ninety-nine out of a hundred people who have never examined it assume that scene fabric is lapped over the edges of frames. Of course it never is, but is pasted to the face of the frame and leaves a little bare wood at all edges. Neither is a continuous straight wall of a room ever made of single flats lashed together, although most amateurs try to make one that way.

For purposes of a representative or pictorial technique scenery is of three kinds; (1) scenery to hang, (2) scenery to bear weight, and (3) scenery to stand. Scenery to hang includes draperies, leg-pieces, cycloramas, drops, borders and ceilings. The director can use draperies, leg-pieces, (the cypress tree mentioned above) and cycloramas. He can use a ceiling if he has facilities for hanging one. Drops and borders are out; they belong to a bygone age. Scenery to bear weight can also be eliminated from the list except for an occasional two- or three-step of stairs, or the skeleton pieces for a Copeau stage.

Scenery to stand is the chief problem. Four-fifths of all scenery in the theatre now stands on its own feet and of this the greater part consists of flats—the elements used for walls. I shall deal with flats first. They are the staff of life of the theatre.

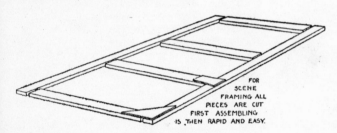

FOR SCENE FRAMING ALL PIECES ARE CUT FIRST ASSEMBLING IS THEN RAPID AND EASY.

FIG. 7. SCENE-FRAMING

It is well to establish at the start the standard height of flats and the standard widths for the various purposes. These measures should be decided upon and after that varied only for the best of reasons. Twelve feet is about the minimum height for flats, fourteen is better, and sixteen is standard in most theatres. The theatre standard width is 5' 9" in order that scene frames will just go in at a box-car door when travelling. For non-professional use a standard width of four feet is better. For faces of pilasters or pillar pieces three feet is best and for the *returns* or *flippers*—the side pieces of a pillar are called by both names—two feet. If the director will thus make up everything in four, three and two foot sizes he will get permutability in his pieces.

Each frame consists of six pieces of dressed pine $\frac{7}{8}''$ thick and three inches (actually as dressed $2\frac{3}{4}''$) wide. The two upright pieces called *stiles*, are the full standard length of the flat. The four cross pieces, called *battens* are four (three or two) feet, less the combined width of the two stiles. The battens are at exact third intervals. (Figure 7). An accurately squared templet or pattern of the standard frame required is marked on the floor

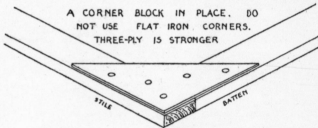

A CORNER BLOCK IN PLACE. DO NOT USE FLAT IRON CORNERS. THREE-PLY IS STRONGER

STILE   BATTEN

AND EASIER. IT WILL SEEM SHAKY UNTIL THE FABRIC IS IN PLACE ON THE OTHER SIDE.

FIG. 8. CORNER-BLOCKING

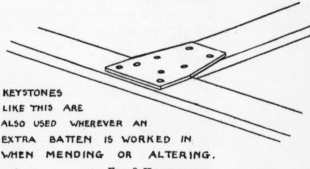

KEYSTONES LIKE THIS ARE ALSO USED WHEREVER AN EXTRA BATTEN IS WORKED IN WHEN MENDING OR ALTERING.

FIG. 9 KEYSTONING

with chalk and the framing pieces laid in place. No mortising or tenoning is needed. The corners are fastened together with corner blocks of 3-ply veneer board set back an inch in the case of pillar faces, and nailed with 1¼" clouts. (Figure 8). Where the two middle battens meet the stiles, keystones of 3-ply are similarly placed. (Figure 9). When the frame is first lifted it will be a bit shaky but the fabric which is to go on the face will correct that. The frame is now ready for covering.

Figures 10, 11 and 12 show the essential processes of covering. The material may be unbleached sheeting of medium weight, or some cheap form of cotton sacking. Avoid burlap except as a special surfacing material to be applied over the cotton. The fabric is laid on the frame with the edge allowed to hang over and is tacked along the *inner* edge of one side, then an end, then the other side and last the other end, keeping it just tight enough

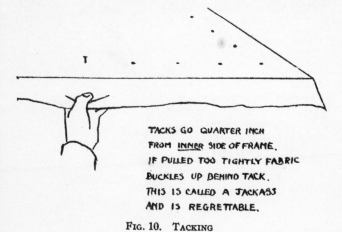

TACKS GO QUARTER INCH
FROM INNER SIDE OF FRAME.
IF PULLED TOO TIGHTLY FABRIC
BUCKLES UP BEHIND TACK.
THIS IS CALLED A JACKASS
AND IS REGRETTABLE.

FIG. 10.   TACKING

to be neat. (Figure 10). The glue on the paint will do some tightening on its own account. Tacking is best done by subdivision, both ends, the middle point, quarters, eights and so on until the tacks are about three

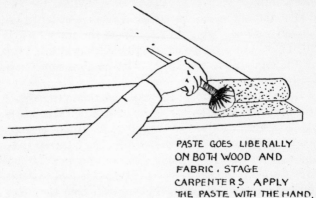

PASTE GOES LIBERALLY ON BOTH WOOD AND FABRIC. STAGE CARPENTERS APPLY THE PASTE WITH THE HAND.

FIG. 11. PASTING

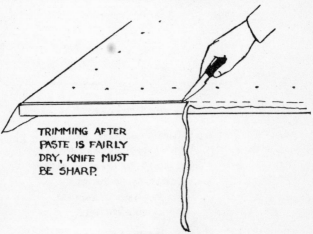

TRIMMING AFTER PASTE IS FAIRLY DRY, KNIFE MUST BE SHARP.

FIG. 12. TRIMMING

inches apart.   A stage carpenter works with a magnetic
tack hammer and a mouthful of tacks, drawing the tacks
from his mouth with the hammer.   A single blow suffices
for each tack.   There is no setting or fiddling with the
tacks and one hand is always free for stretching the cloth.
Magnetic tack hammers are inexpensive and there are
always applicants for a job where they are used.

The fabric is then pasted with flour paste made with
boiling water or with stick-fast and cold water, (Figure
11) rubbed down on the wood and laid away to dry.
When it is dry, or nearly so, the carpenter trims away
the superfluous cloth with a knife, running his knife-line
about a quarter of an inch from the edge of the frame.
(Figure 12).   This is for *single* flats used separately or
hinged into right-angled elements of any sort.

Where a flat is to form part of a continuous wall two
frames are hinged up into a double element or what is
called a simple book.   The pieces are hinged as in Figure
13c and a sewn piece of fabric is laid over the whole face.
Some paste and a few tacks are put in on the inner stiles
for luck.   Two-way right-angle hinging (Figure 13b) is
used for a variety of purposes and is extremely useful for
changing elements where a new arrangement is necessary.
It requires two singly-covered flats.   Pilasters and pillar
pieces are hinged one way and at right angles (Figure 13d
and 13e).   In the case of a three-foot face and two two-
foot returns or flippers one of the sides will require to be
hinged with a *dutchman*, to allow of flat folding.   A
dutchman is a long piece of pine $7/8$ by $7/8$ inches, and is
as shown in the drawing. The width of the dutchman
should not be deducted from the flipper, but hinged to it.
The extra inch is not visible to an audience and the
standard width of flats for other uses is maintained.

PIN HINGING WITH
PIN WIRE THIS
IS USED ALSO FOR
FASTENING ONE
PIECE TO ANOTHER.

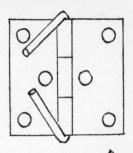

A

STIFFENERS FOR THE BACKS OF
SCENERY, JACKS USED AS
BRACES, WINDOW THICKNESSES
SHOULD ALL BE PIN HINGED
IN A SELF RESPECTING THEATRE.

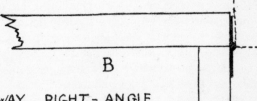

B

TWO WAY RIGHT - ANGLE
HINGING. THE ONLY DISAD-
VANTAGE OF THIS IS THAT
FOR PACKING THE PIN WIRE
(BENT WIRE) MUST BE TAKEN
OUT EACH TIME.

FIG. 13 HINGING

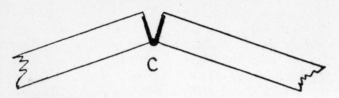

SIMPLE HINGING   ALWAYS
PUT HINGE ON THE EDGE OF
STYLE   NEVER ON FACE   USE
LOOSE PIN HINGE AND RE-
PLACE PIN WITH WIRE.

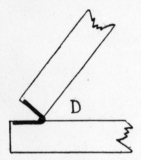
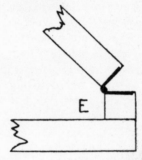

ONE WAY RIGHT-   ONE WAY RIGHT-
ANGLE HINGING   ANGLE HINGING
ON PILASTER.   WITH DUTCHMAN
            TO LET E. FOLD OVER D.

Fig. 13a

Hinges should all be at standard heights from the floor so
as to be interchangeable. Loose pin $\frac{3}{4}''$ steel butt
hinges should be used and a piece of wire substituted for
the pin as in Figure 13a. They will then come apart
when wanted and otherwise will hold. Pin hinges are to
a showman what a needle and thread are to the house-
wife.

In the preceding section, discussing interior elements
for pictorial scenery I spoke of an arrangement of pieces
which will give the umost use at the least cost. On a
basis of four-foot-standard flats, three-foot pillar pieces
with two-foot returns, a complete outfit capable of making interiors for almost any production of three acts or
under, would consist of eight fours (two-way right-angle
hinged into four elements), eight fours (simple-hinged into
four elements) four pillar pieces of three flats each, and
four single pieces for cutting into windows and doors.
This is a total of twenty fours, four threes and eight twos
or thirty two frames hinged into sixteen elements. The
director will be foolish to buy all these at the start, unless
he has a fairy godmother, but he will be wise to make such
a set his objective and collect the necessary pieces as he
goes, making each show contribute two or three to his
stock, until at last he can move indoors from his frag-
mentary and atmospheric exteriors with a real house to
play in.

I hope he understands about scenery that it never
has texture until it has been covered with paint half a
dozen times. To make a scene he should assemble the
required elements into the plan he desires regardless of
what ghosts of past plays are visible on their surface,
give them a sweep of ground colour and proceed with his
decorative scheme. The only people who believe in new

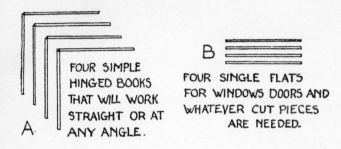

FOUR SIMPLE
HINGED BOOKS
THAT WILL WORK
STRAIGHT OR AT
ANY ANGLE.

A

FOUR SINGLE FLATS
FOR WINDOWS DOORS AND
WHATEVER CUT PIECES
ARE NEEDED.

B

C_ FOUR PILLAR PIECES EACH WITH A DUTCHMAN. (D)
THESE FOR PILASTERS AND JOGS. THE FLIPPER PIECES
. MARKED (F) CAN BE BORROWED FOR OTHER USES.

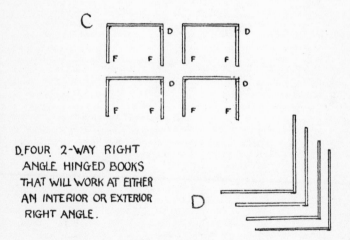

D. FOUR 2-WAY RIGHT
ANGLE HINGED BOOKS
THAT WILL WORK AT EITHER
AN INTERIOR OR EXTERIOR
RIGHT ANGLE.

FIG. 14.   A FAMILY OF INTERIOR ELEMENTS

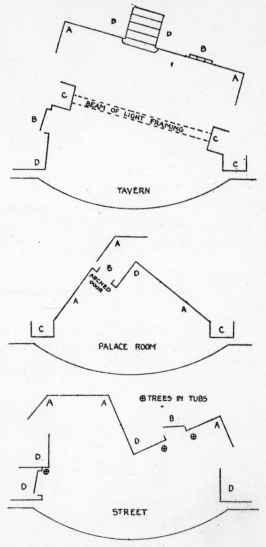

FIG. 15. THREE SCENES MADE FROM THE ELEMENTS

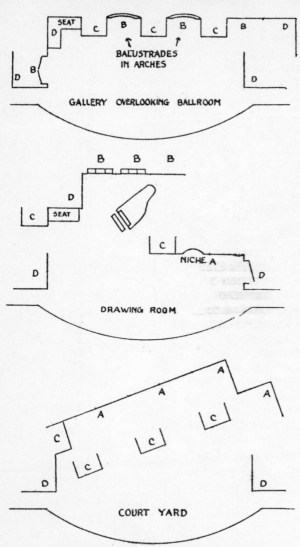

GALLERY OVERLOOKING BALLROOM

DRAWING ROOM

COURT YARD

FIG. 16. THREE MORE SCENES

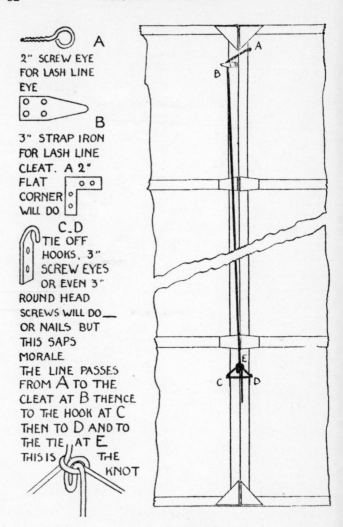

A

2" SCREW EYE
FOR LASH LINE
EYE

B

3" STRAP IRON
FOR LASH LINE
CLEAT. A 2"
FLAT
CORNER
WILL DO

C_D
TIE OFF
HOOKS, 3"
SCREW EYES
OR EVEN 3"
ROUND HEAD
SCREWS WILL DO___
OR NAILS BUT
THIS SAPS
MORALE
THE LINE PASSES
FROM A TO THE
CLEAT AT B THENCE
TO THE HOOK AT C
THEN TO D AND TO
THE TIE AT E
THIS IS   THE
                 KNOT

FIG. 17.   LASHING UP

scenery are those who sell it. Figure 14 shows the family of elements singly and Figures 15 and 16 show them arranged in a few of their possible interrelations. It will be seen that frequently a flat is allowed to stand off-stage and out of sight. This is for bracing and if the flat can be spared is an excellent practice.

Little other bracing of scenery is needed if the joints are securely lashed up. Lashing up is done as in Figure 17 with a piece of clothes line or, better, with the braided rope known commercially as "trick line"—a trifle smaller than sash cord. The line is fastened to a lash-line-eye a foot from the top of the stile of the left hand frame. At fourteen inches from the top of the stile of the right hand is a lash cleat of flat iron. A flat-corner set on the face of the wood as in the drawing will do. The line is snapped over the lash cleat and pulled down to a left-hand tie-off which may be a round-headed screw, then passed under the right hand tie-off, then secured as in the drawing, so that it can be released in an instant. The tie-off should be a standard two feet six inches from

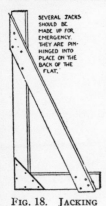

SEVERAL JACKS SHOULD BE MADE UP FOR EMERGENCY. THEY ARE PIN-HINGED INTO PLACE ON THE BACK OF THE FLAT.

Fig. 18. Jacking

the floor. No other point of contact is needed except these four unless the flat is badly warped. One eye, one cleat and two tie-offs. When the piece is out of use and is to be struck away the line is passed behind the lower batten and caught in a slipknot.

In the few cases where such a scene as I have described needs bracing it can be done with jacks which are right-angle triangles of wood about three feet high and eighteen inches on the foot. (Figure 18).

They should be pin-hinged to the flat they brace and should stay with it. The easiest way to secure them to the floor is to throw a heavy sandbag across the toe.

Patching, joining and altering scene frames is rarely more than a few minute's work. To patch a hole, cut an irregular piece of fabric and paste it on the face of the flat. Then paint as if there were no break, and the patch will disappear. To join two flats into a simple book so that the joint will not show, hinge them together and paste a piece of cotton about ten inches wide down the crack. This will also paint out and become invisible. Altering a frame, to put in, let us say, a window, requires that the flat be thrown face downward on the floor, the necessary batten and stile pieces keystoned into place and the unwanted fabric cut roughly away. The piece is then turned over, the cloth tacked as for screen covering and the edges pasted and trimmed. See Figure 19.

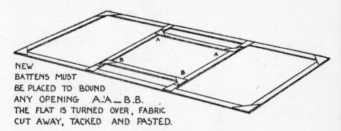

NEW BATTENS MUST BE PLACED TO BOUND ANY OPENING A.'A — B.B. THE FLAT IS TURNED OVER, FABRIC CUT AWAY, TACKED AND PASTED.

FIG. 19. ALTERING AND MENDING

Thicknesses on windows and doors are essential to good scenery. It is better to go through a gap in the wall and pretend that the door is down a corridor than have those silly little flappy doors of a few years ago. A door or window thickness for school or little theatre use, where the scenery does not have to travel is merely a box

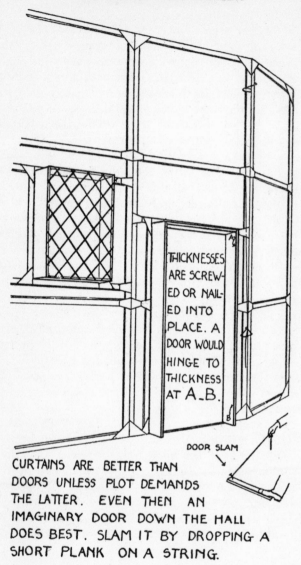

THICKNESSES ARE SCREWED OR NAILED INTO PLACE. A DOOR WOULD HINGE TO THICKNESS AT A_B.

DOOR SLAM

CURTAINS ARE BETTER THAN DOORS UNLESS PLOT DEMANDS THE LATTER. EVEN THEN AN IMAGINARY DOOR DOWN THE HALL DOES BEST. SLAM IT BY DROPPING A SHORT PLANK ON A STRING.

FIG. 20. THICKNESSES

of $\frac{7}{8}$" dressed stuff about eight inches wide (Figure 20) affixed to the back of the frame and taken off and broken up when done with. A window or door should be fixed to the back of this thickness. The bottom of a door or arch needs something to keep it rigid. This should be a wooden sill the same width as a thickness, and chamfered or levelled so that the actor will not trip. Where curved openings or soffits of arches have to be thicknessed it may be easily done with sheet metal, but never with beaver-board. The sheet metal can be nailed to the edge of the wood and will always look neat.

A theatre ceiling should be avoided if possible. It is not hard to make but it is hard to hang in most halls. If there is an ordinarily high ceiling over the playing space the scenery should be made to come within two or three inches of it. The gap will never show. If the ceiling is irregular or too high all that is necessary is to paint an arbitrary black band six inches wide around the top of all scenes and the spectator's eye will stop there unless there is light above it. If the director must have a ceiling it is made by laying out on the floor a piece of cloth sewn to the necessary size, affixing a batten along each of the long sides of it and then nailing or screwing down on them transverse stretcher-pieces which will force out the battens, thus pulling the cloth tight. The cloth is never nailed to the stretchers but allowed to belly down a little. The ends are then tacked lightly to the end stretchers, the whole frame is turned over, and the ceiling painted. In the theatre it is hung on two sets of three lines each, a back set fastened to the upstage batten and a "trip" set fastened to the downstage batten. The director who has to use one will find it better to hinge it to his back wall, so that it will drop out of the way when not in use, and raise it on a trip-set only. It must be lifted a foot or more every time a scene is changed. The greatest service of a ceiling is that it locks scene elements into place when it is resting on them.

Solid pieces of all sorts are best made roughly of any odds and ends of wood to a close approximation of the shape required— paying no attention to patching or finish—and covered with coarse sacking or burlap which is first tacked to make it secure. The fabric is then "doped" into place with a thick mixture of whiting and glue. This affords a fine base for paint. In modern practice all heavy properties, tree trunks, balustrades, steps, statuary, fountains, sundials, chests, thrones, garden-seats, relief work, pillars and pieces with mouldings are roughly carpentered and given their finish by "doping". A few experiments will give the necessary skill, and beautiful scene-pieces can be achieved. Some directors burlap the surface of flats in the same way with quarter-inch-mesh plasterer's sacking, thereby getting fine texture and a honeycombed surface for light.

Scene painting has undergone many reforms in recent years and the elaborate, naturalistic painting is rapidly disappearing for both interiors and exteriors. The old painted landscape painted on a back cloth is scarcely ever seen in good work. Its place is taken by the blue, lighted cyclorama. Wood-wings, which were just flats with a foliage edge, are extinct, and foliage borders will soon be in their long last resting-place with oak-beam, sky, kitchen and drawing-room fancy borders.

Painting is confined to the application of their natural colours to walls, tree-trunks, architectural exedra and properties, and to the application of pattern. Texture is secured by the processes of sponging or ragging. The practice in the treatment of interior walls is now to lay on a ground coat with a large brush. Then taking a carriage-sponge dipped in another colour and squeezed out a little, to apply a stipple to the entire surface. A third colour is then stippled on and perhaps a fourth, with care that the predominant hue desired is the last to be laid on. Necessary skirtings, patterns and moulding lines are applied with a small brush. There are few of the old burnt umber and raw sienna shadows, none of the panel and fancy shadows. Pattern is often secured by working the sponge with the hand into an attractive shape and sponging at intervals with that. Wall-paper is very easily suggested in this way.

Ragging is the same as sponging except that a large crumpled rag is used. It requires a little more address and on account of its bigger accidents of pattern is preferred for exterior stucco walls.

On properly textured walls, however, light is the great colourist and after the director has pulled his elements together with a neutral ground coat he should see what his light will give him before he wastes time painting. Curtains and wall ornaments, such as pictures, tapestries and rugs, will often give him all the high pigment colour he needs without further effort.

All stage painting is done with "water colour" or distemper. Oil colour is not used because it will strike through any water colour applied over it. If oil does get on a scene by accident the place should be shellacked before water-colour is applied.

Distemper consists of ground glue, whiting and water, The glue should be melted in water over a stove and when it is hot, added to the whiting and water which have been previously mixed to the consistency of thin cream. About a pint of melted glue to an iron bucket of water and whiting makes a stiff mixture. The whole bucket should now be set on a stove and brought almost to a boil, stirring it to mix in the glue. This is the base for all colours. The dry pigment is then added as desired, and hot water put in if thinning is necessary. The pigment range for distemper is not wide. Many colours that would survive in oil are reduced to a pastel tint by the whiting required to give body to distemper. The scene painter relies chiefly on the following dry colours for his palette: Reds—English Vermilion, Indian, Turkey, and Venetian: Blues—Ultramarine, Italian, Prussian and Cobalt: Greens—Malachite, Prussian, Chrome and Emerald: Yellows:—Chrome, Ochre and Dutch Pink (an extremely useful mustard hue): Oranges—Chrome: Purples—Purple Lake (bluish) and Chatamuk Lake (reddish); Black—Lamp Black; Browns —Raw Umber, Burnt Umber, Burnt Sienna and Vandyke Brown: Whites—Whiting, as described above.

Whiting gives the distemper its covering power. When the white has interfered too much with the hue of the painted surface, the latter may be vivified by "glazing" with a mixture of thin glue and pure colour. After scenery has been painted many times there is already enough glue in it. A little pigment in hot water will therefore do for glazing. A thin glaze of the sort is sometimes drawn over an entire scene to harmonize jarring elements in its colour.

A patch of colour may also be modified by "dragging" over it a nearly dry brush containing another colour. This is also called "scumbling" and the modifying colour appears in small streaks and patches.

"Dope" for affixing sacking to a scene piece is the

same as distemper except that it requires a little more glue and about twice as much whiting. It is applied with a brush and is worked in with the hands.

I append here a few hints that will prove useful:

In sponging, do not do a flat at a time, but work across several flats in the relative positions they will occupy and carry the stippling in big circular sweeps. Otherwise the pieces may not match.

Do not bother to glue-size scenery before painting it. There is enough size in the paint to do all that is required.

If a pigment is of very light weight it will not mix readily in water. Lamp black is the worst offender. A dash of methylated spirit or a little shellac thrown in the water will digest the pigment immediately.

Never fuss with scenery. Work broadly and always leave out a process rather than do one too many. Half the things done on scenery never show. Lay it down on the floor and walk back and forward over it to apply paint. A colour may be spattered on with a brush and sponged when it begins to dry.

All newly painted scenery looks too crisp and fresh. It needs what is called "breaking down." This is done by eliminating edges and corners with a fairly dry sponge dipped in a neutral or darker colour—gray, brown, tan, or gray-blue as the scene requires. Scenery is at its best when its decorative elements have a circular quality with corners and tops and bottoms of walls reduced in wide curved sweeps. The reader will see what I mean by studying a Brangwyn painting.

Built and painted scenery is used also in the Copeau method but obviously it cannot be standardized to the same degree. Pillars and tall flats are employed and are afterwards broken up and converted to new needs.

There is scarcely any limit to the number of times stage scenery can be made over in a Copeau scene. It does not have to be shifted so need have no more strength than will keep it upright when it is nailed into place.

V. PROCESSES AND MATERIALS

A LL crafts in the theatre are based on a "look-like"
technique.   They are none the less good art on this
account.   Only an appearance is needed and it would
be bad art to go a hair's breadth beyond that.   Art is
something one does, not something one possesses to put
on the mantel shelf.   In the theatre which, like music,
exists for the moment there is no virtue in the actuality
of an object, although many people still think there is.

The skill of a theatre technician consists in his ability
to get an effect at small cost and with speed and certainty,
He is on the watch therefore for simple processes and
materials that will give him the results he needs.   A few
of these which will be of use to a director should have a
place here.

One of the most valuable materials of recent arrival
in the theatre is burlap, the quarter and eighth inch mesh
sacking used by plaster casters for strengthening their
work.   It costs four to eight dollars a hundred yards
and to get this price one must buy it in the hundred yard
bolt.   For massive drapes, for tree effects, for legs and
masking pieces it may be used in its natural colour or
may be sprayed with, or dipped in, aniline.   At a
distance it approximates velvet.   The greatest use however for the sacking is for the "doping" process I have
described.

Aniline dyes are extremely useful in the theatre.
They cost twenty-five cents an ounce and are so strong
that a very little will give a rich tint.   The fact
that many of them are fugitive to sunlight does not

matter in the theatre. Some are soluble in alcohol and some in water. The first should be avoided. The best anilines soluble in water are Walnut Brown, Bismarck Brown, Yellow, Blue, Red and Malachite Green. These all mix freely for intermediate hues and may be supplemented by the use of the ordinary package dyes, which however are in comparison about ten times as expensive as well as having a residuum of mud. Fly screen or wire cloth (galvanized; not black or green) is used for glass, especially for stained glass windows. It is stretched on a frame and any seams required made by lapping one edge over the other and sewing or lacing tight with a ravelling of the wire. It is then painted *on both sides* at the same time, with a hot solution of uncoloured cooking gelatine. The leading is then traced in with flat-black oil colour and the coloured quarries filled in with a mixture of hot gelatine and the required hue of aniline. Such a window is luminous and brilliant.

Small mesh chicken wire is used for grills and frets in windows and doors. The wire mesh is stretched to its frame and the pattern traced with chalk. Wood-flour and paste is then worked into the interstices where the design requires it. The design is then painted with black or a metal bronze powder of any colour. Beautiful pierced-work lattices and filigree lamps can be approximated in this medium. The wood flour is purchaseable from a pulp mill or from a doll manufacturer. The same consistency of material can be secured by boiling newspapers until they are resolved into a pulpy mass.

Papier mâché working is one of the most valuable of the crafts of the theatre and a director contemplating regular work will do well to set one or two of his people at it to learn its intricacies. Papier mâché is used for armour, helmets, masks, animal heads and a host of objects that have to be of modelled surface and light in weight. If the article is small and solid it can be made of wood-flour or newspaper-pulp, mixed with paste and can be modelled directly with the fingers, where the object must be hollow, or where several casts are required a mould should be made and strawboard used. The first step is to model the object in clay as it is to appear from the outside. From this a plaster mould is taken just as in plaster casting. It may be a single mould or a piece mould. The worker should consult a book on plaster casting for the detail of this process of taking the mould. After the mould is made it should be shellacked inside and oiled with boiled linseed oil. Next comes the laying in of the paper. This is the thickest variety of strawboard torn into a convenient size and allowed to soak for half an hour in a wash-boiler full of water. When taken out the paper is drained of free water and torn into irregular pieces about six by eight inches in size. The trick in all papier mâché work is to split these pieces, and, tearing them to a convenient size to fit the irregularities of the mould, to press them, overlapping a little, firmly into place. The patches can be made to lie evenly if they are torn a trifle at intervals along their edges and at right angles to it. As each piece is laid in place a liberal amount of paste is rubbed into it. Less care need be taken with the second layer. The pieces need not be split but their edges should be torn as before. The excellence of papier mâché is in direct proportion to the care which the paper is pressed into the mould. The finishing of the edges is as follows: The first or split layer is allowed to project an inch or two beyond the edge of the mould. The second and third layers are cut off even with the edge. The projecting flap is then turned over and firmly pasted down. In a helmet or any article made in a piece mould of two or more parts all edges are done the same whether they are to be seams in the finished work or not. The edges which are to be seams will come together as the pieces of the mould come together. They require however to be reinforced from the inside with well-pasted patches. When the mould is locked its parts are bound together with rope or rags and the operator reaching inside of it affixes the reinforcing patches lapping one over another all along the seams. The form, as the papier mâché cast is called, is now ready to dry. If paperhanger's paste is used it can be dried in 6 to 8 hours, by putting it near heat. The form is removed before it is quite dry and the external seams are covered with patches of split paper. All loose pieces are pasted down and the form allowed to dry without heat. One form a day without artificial heat gives the best results. If rapid heat is required an electric light bulb may be put inside the mould.

Helmet and armour forms should be worked up in bronze powder of which there are over thirty colours available. They should never be done in one colour or the actors will look like animated radiators. All the high lights should be scumbled over a dark base. Metallic stove blacking is the best black and should be rubbed in with a brush. The media for bronze powders are banana oil or (preferably) Japan dyers. For giving the high glints to helmets or armour the bronze can be applied with a rag. Papier mâché should always be shellacked before being painted.

Bronze powders have many uses in the theatre. The colour of distemper may be heightened by scattering a little bronze of the same hue on the top of the bucket full of paint and allowing it to adhere to the brush. If the powder is mixed with the distemper its zest is lost.

Plaster-working *in situ*, or the process of modelling directly in plaster instead of casting it, is a fascinating craft and is suited to many kinds of properties, especially gold and silver table ornaments, caskets, hand-mirrors, urns, and many other small objects. Where a director has two or three young women available and desires to give them work not too heavy for them he should provide for plaster modelling. The medium—plaster of paris—is mixed with water as for plaster casting, with the difference that the water is first mixed with dextrine, a tablespoonful to a washbasin of water. This retards the setting of the plaster. Sugar or glue in the same proportions may be substituted for the dextrine. The basin is first filled with water and the plaster dropped in, a handful at a time, and allowed to sink in. No rubbish or lumps should be permitted in the mixture, nor should the latter be stirred until there has been put in all the plaster the water will digest. It may then be stirred, agitating the lower part of the mixture as much, and the upper as little, as possible until the mass is homogenized. The plaster should then be applied to an armature or form studded with bent nails. The armature should be first shellacked or glue-sized. The modelling is done with the fingers, with modelling tools, or in the last stages, with a plasterer's riffler. Plaster mixed with dextrine, sugar or glue is very tough and will withstand considerable rough usage. Salt is used to hasten the setting of plaster when a quick cast is needed.

Beaver board is only useful within limits. It should never be used for scenery unless perhaps for cut-out trees against a cyclorama. It is hard to cut neatly and for most purposes is thoroughly unworkmanlike. It is also frail and goes to pieces in handling. Cottonwood three-ply, now made in large quantities and available all over, is far better. For cut-outs a frame should be made as for any other scenery and the three-ply laid on and allowed to project to the desired outline. This is true also of all profiling, as the irregular outline of roof-tops, wall-edges and the like is called in the theatre.

Hedges, pleached trees, and all garden decorations can best be made by constructing a rough framework of wood, and stretching or pleating plasterer's sacking over it in several thicknesses. The sacking is then sprayed with aniline with an air-brush. Malachite green and a little lamp-black makes a good mixture for shrubbery. As the liquid in the container diminishes, the colour will grow darker. This dark pigment should be used for irregular patches to give life to the surface.

The air-brush is invaluable for stage decoration. It is run by compressed air and will project any kind of liquid. The best variety of brush is the sturdy lacquer-gun of commercial use attached to a drum of air or to a garage compressor. The mixture is made in any container and the suction tube of the gun is thrust into it. Self-colour or pattern can be sprayed to cover wide areas in a few minutes. serviceable gun costs about twelve dollars and a hand compressor can be had for fifteen. When compressed air is not available the carbonic gas tanks supplied to soda fountains will do. The released carbonic gas makes the gun intensely cold and the operator had better provide himself with mittens.

Stencils may be used for applying patterns to walls, curtains, or dresses.   There is a prepared stencil paper at art stores but it is better for the worker to make his own out of cartoon paper or heavy wrapping paper.   The pattern is outlined, the paper coated, both sides, with boiled oil and allowed to wait overnight to dry.   It is then laid on a sheet of glass and cut with a sharp knife. In the finished work on the wall or fabric the stencil ties should not be painted out.   They give vigour to the design.   Any of the prepared show-card colours will work on fabric, or distemper may be used.   After stencilling, the fabric should be carefully ironed to take out the puckers.

VI. COSTUME AND MAKE-UP

IN SO small a hand-book I have no space for more than general observations on costume. I can best serve the director by suggesting the mood in which this department of his work should be undertaken and offer a few practical hints on method.

Costume should from the first be the province of one person in the director's group and the latter will do well to pass over a very expert and assured person for another with less experience but with more capacity for learning as the work proceeds. A costume worker who knows everything at the start can seriously impair the whole venture. Theatre costume is not fancy dress, neither is it masquerade apparel. It is made according to canons of its own. It is never so carefully finished, it requires to be much more emphatic in its design and pattern, and it should be made out of much coarser and cheaper material than the average miss would care to wear to a party.

The designer's first task is to catch the spirit of the production and then make every costume conform to it. A dress for the theatre is never something for itself: it is always a part of a greater whole and must partake of the emphasis and style of the whole. Sometimes the necessary exaggerations of a production will be in the cloaks, sometimes in the sleeves, sometimes in the breeches and sometimes in the flare of skirted coats. The designer should never make slavish copies of appropriate figures in costume books, one by one, until his list of characters is filled. If his play is one of cloaks he should go in for cloaks in all their expressive forms; if it is one of slim eel-like figures he should dress them in hose, tight little tunics and by-cocket hats or perky little close-fitting caps. If it is a play of beggars in rags and tatters he should design in tatters, and never in finished dresses that are to be tattered after they are made. If he strives thus for a general harmony he need not fear too great sameness. Variety will creep in without any effort on his part. If, however, he starts out for variety he will get nothing but incongruity.

The most important quality of a fabric—more important even than its colour—is its characteristic way of hanging and folding. Having found the material that suits the play the designer will do well to use it as much as possible throughout. Ratine, cotton-crepe, cashmerette, felt, cheap dress-goods have all characters of their own and each can usually be found in a sufficiently wide family of colours to meet most demands of a play. Hue is important but there are so many ways of modifying or heightening an unsatisfactory hue by means of painted pattern, by *applique*, by "dragging" with a metallic powder, and by metal ornament that the hue of a fabric should never be allowed to tempt the designer off his course, either into extravagance or into getting one materal that will not consort with the others. All richness of costume on stage is comparative and a peculiarly attractive fabric must not be allowed to reveal the humble quality of the others.

The designer should never make more of a dress than actually shows in the scene. Unless it happens to be the plot of the play, we have no interest in how a Roman put on his clothes in the morning. We care only how they looked when he had them on, and then only through the eyes of the best contemporary artists. A Roman in a toga is for purposes of the theatre, an actor in a toga, with no more between him and the toga than will keep him respectable and warm. A richly brocaded waistcoat is two narrow strips of something that at twenty feet or more will look like rich brocade, and whether they are fastened to his shirt or to the inside of his coat is determined entirely by the actor's convenience If the wearer must take his snuff-box from the pocket of it, one of the narrow strips will have to be a broad strip with a pocket. The designer who can remember this and not wander into the pleasant fields of archaeology will save his group much time and money. The theatre offers a great schooling in elimination.

Careful pressing, not only before the dress rehearsal but between performances as well, is half the battle in good theatre dressing.   The folds in garments for the stage can be much sharper and pleats should be well defined. Even the distortion of garments caused in life by hard wear must never be allowed to *happen*. They should be made.   It is a common error to suppose that a peasant's clothes will be all right if they look as if they came out of the rag bag. The pouches in the knees of the trousers should be worked up by pulling the cloth, then rubbing well with vaseline and the shine taken off if necessary with dry pigment mixed to the proper colour and thoroughly rubbed in. All well-worn garments should be sculptural and should reveal the figure.

The dressmaker will find necessary uses for shiny fabrics like sateen, Roman satin, mercerized goods as well as for the book-muslins so dear to the cantata costumier. She may even find a place for gold and silver paper but none of these should be used except in the last extremity.

They are insincere and unconvincing fabrics and take
light badly.

Wigs for costume plays present great difficulties for
amateur groups but the use of caps will solve most problems.   The old painters show scores of interesting shapes
that can be made out of old felt hats or sewn felt, suited
to both young and old characters.   Short curls or a fringe
of white crepe-hair sewn to the edge of such a cap will
give all that a wig can.

Crepe-hair should be used for all beards.   The wired
contrivances that hook over the ears should never be
permitted on a stage   The director of a school group
should set one of his people to work on beard making and
let him do all the beard work for the company.

The first process in laying a beard is to stretch out a
piece of crepe-hair free of the string on which it is braided
and cut off twelve inches of it.   Then making sure that
the strands of hair are parallel and straight, "fluff" it
out into a flat mat.   This is a rather tricky operation
and must be done very carefully with the thumbs and
first fingers in such a way as to keep the mat from
twisting and to avoid making long rents and thin places
in the piece.   The mat should be five inches wide when
it is finished and perfectly even in texture.   The experi-
menter may expect to spoil the first two or three pieces.
The entire lower part of the face of the actor should be
brushed over with spirit gum—gum arabic dissolved in
grain-alcohol—and the spirit allowed to evaporate.   A
shallow V is then cut in one end of the mat and the V put
against the actor's throat and firmly affixed to the under
side of his chin by pressing it with a wrung-out towel held
bandage-wise.   The other end of the mat should now be
clipped into the outline of a W and applied to the front

of the chin so that the tongue of the W comes under the lower lip and the two wings at the ends of the mouth. This should be pressed with the wet towel. The beard so far hangs in a loop open at the sides. Two long tapering pieces running from half an inch to two inches wide are now affixed to the cheeks in front of the ears, pressed into place and the ends neatly tucked into the sides of the loop. The entire beard is now caught together with needle and thread and patted into shape. A mustache, consisting of a thin strand is laid along the upper lip and trained down into the mat. After placing it, sever the mustache at the middle to free the actor's mouth muscles. Loose hairs at the cut edges are trimmed away with scissors or gummed down to the skin. All full beards, long or short and of whatever cut are modifications of this. If a peculiarly thick beard is desired the loop should be cut at the bottom and another mat of hair fixed in between the upper and lower mats.

The little chin beards, Judas beards, Jaques beards and the like are laid on with thin strands of crepe-hair. Care must be taken not to use much hair in these. The operator must always use the wet towel for pressing. Once his fingers get gummed his usefulness is at an end until he washes them thoroughly. He, may, indeed, overcome the gum on his fingers temporarily with talcum but an artist never lets his fingers touch the gum.

Well made beards are of the greatest importance in a school theatre and no trouble is too great that will give clean-cut results. Especially with young players is it necessary to get a convincing indication of maturity or old age and no other device is so satisfacrory as a well modelled beard. Crepe hair can be made straight by laying it away over night in a damp towel but the crinkley kind is best and most durable. If carefully removed, beards can be used two or three times. It is, however, poor economy to use them after they have become stringy or ragged.

Facial make-up is not the difficult thing so many people make of it and can be easily learned if a few principles are kept in mind. The first is that the face should first be rubbed with cold cream and then wiped clean. It should next be powdered with face powder, and a powdering should follow every operation, the powder being wiped carefully each time so that no surplus remains. The ground tone for straight make-up should be laid evenly over the whole face. Except for young girls it should never be pink, but always a good tan or sunburn with an admixture of yellow. Yellow in stage lights gives transparency and vigour to the skin. The cheek colour may now be laid in, pulling it pretty evenly over the whole cheek for men, and high up on the cheek bones and under the eyes for women. The eyebrows should now be accentuated with a dark pencil and the line of each eyelash marked carefully. There should be a little dark colour on each eyelid at the outside, a line at each side, to lengthen the eye a little, and a touch of carmine at the inner end of each eye to give brilliancy. Carmine may now be put on the lips and a little in each nostril. Powder again.

For old age make-up more reliance must be placed on dress, hair, beard, walk and gesture than upon the intricate fine lines which actors have hitherto used to mark their faces. Lines of old age should be very few and for the most part should be accentuations of the wrinkles in the face. Far better than a mesh of crow's feet is to darken the whole hollow of the eye with a light brown or a light blue. The deep lines down from the nose to the ends of the mouth may be marked more deeply and the colour left out of the lips. A deepening of the horizontal line between mouth and chin is of use on a bare face. For every line or depression the make-up man should accentuate the corresponding high places with a little white grease-paint or a pigment of a higher tint.

The director will do well to give the whole make-up problem to one of his aides and allow him to specialize in it. With the proper tools he can make up the entire company in half an hour to an hour. He will not only get better results but he will secure a fifty per-cent saving in paints and other make-up necessities. All of the requirements for make-up can be bought from any druggist, who if he already does not carry a stock can soon get in touch with one of the many supply houses. All make-up should be assumed as a cost of the production and everything kept by the make-up man.

VII. STAGE LIGHTING

RECENT advances in the art of stage lighting have conspired more to the advantage of the non-professional than have any of the other advances in the theatre. A few years ago when the gradual evolution of footlights and borders through the successive stages of candles, lamps, gas, carbon incandescents and Mazdas had reached its climax in the nitrogen lamp, the possibility of getting a comparable effect to that of the commercial theatre was beyond the means of a small organization. It did not occur to most amateurs that they did not require a comparable effect so they rigged up tin troughs for footlights and overhead reflector strips for borderlights but real flood-lighting was impossible except in the crudest way.

Now the theatre, through the agency of amateurs who were wiser than to imitate flood-lighting, has turned to what is called point lighting, and with the smaller room in his favour the school theatre director can get at small expense all the professional director gets.

Point lighting is in its simplest form, the illumination of the actor from the natural light source. If he is sitting at a table near a lighted lamp the lamp does the lighting. If he is near a window the light pouring in at the window is the illuminant. Noonday sunlight falls from directly overhead, morning or evening sunlight from one side or the other, moonlight from anywhere above as the action requires.

In a very small auditorium nothing more would be required any more than it is required in a house or out of doors in the sunlight. But because an audience is especially interested in the face of an actor, and because no director is skilful enough to keep all his faces in the direction of the light source all the time the audience is interested in them, it becomes desirable in the ordinary hall, and imperative in the theatre that the faces be "picked up" from the spectator's side and the harsh shadows softened a little or it will happen that the face of an actor who turns away from the sun or the lamp will by contrast be lost entirely. There are a few occasions in a serious piece where this disappearance of the actor's face is useful but scarcely ever is it permissible in comedy. The method used, then, to heighten the face lighting and to reduce the contrasts, or to intensify the illumination at a given point—any of the three or all may be necessary—is to hang, just above the proscenium, small hooded lamps of not too great intensity, and aim them to cover the required fields. If, for instance, the scene is a room in evening with the family assembled around a shaded table lamp the practice is to "ring" the table with one or more proscenium lamps, thus heightening the radiance of the ostensible source of light in the room. A couch at a distance will have, if conditions permit, a stand or piano lamp similarly "ringed". If the stand lamp is not permissible, a ringed glow from the fireplace may do it, or lacking this the actor on the couch may be picked up with a lamp without excuse, care taken however that the light be colder in tone than that at the table. Where much movement is required it is the practice to make numerous little pools of light so that the actor is never out of one or other of them. Criss-crossed as they are they never register as patches of light but as a live, delicate illumination that does all that is required of light without obtruding itself. Every problem is met as the table lamp one was. Moonlight pouring in at a window is the same and so are all the forms of exterior lighting. In order to give zest to this pooling of the light the director uses a wide range of colours, not neglecting green which has in light as it has in foliage the property of restoring balance and harmonizing jarring hues. Neither should the director neglect white light as derived from a "daylight" lamp. It is most valuable of all.

For small auditorium use, almost any lamp with a reflector that concentrates the rays will serve for stage-lighting. The lamp in its housing should never have a beam of wider angle than forty-five degrees and twenty degrees is better. Almost any of the scores of reflectors on the market will do and failing them a lamp can be enclosed in a short sleeve of stove pipe that will cut down the angle of its ray. To get a reflecting background in such a lamp housing it is only necessary to paint the inside with Japan dryers and cover the surface liberally with aluminum flitter or dutch-metal except for an inch back from its edge where it should be flat black. Ordinary aluminum paint is not much good. White paint is better.

The best housing for little theatre use is the baby lens lamp used in theatres. It is a sheet iron box about 7 by 7 by 7 inches, well ventilated and fitted with a silvered reflector and a glass condenser. It is usually of non-focussing type and gives a strong but soft illumination. A lamp in the theatre is said to be soft when it does not throw a ring of light but only a glow with no well-defined edges. Baby lens-lamps may be procured from any theatre electrician and when new should not cost over fifteen dollars each. They may be had second-hand for much less. They are lamped with small 100-watt condensed-filament globular bulbs obtainable through any electrical dealer.

Stage lighting is not difficult although much nonsense is talked about the intricacy of it. The fundamentals can be learned in an afternoon. There is, however, no limit to the artistry which may be obtained by patience and experiment, even with the most primitive machinery. Stage lighting is still anybody's game. Most of the elaborate mechanisms of our theatre are mere vanity and are already on their way to the junk heap. The immense quantity of lighting apparatus in the big theatres is rendered necessary by the great distance of the farthest spectator and by the need for flexibility and ease in handling. Stripped to essentials it is nothing but a multiplication of a single unit: a housed bulb, a switch to put it on and off and a dimmer to control its intensity. Dimmers can be bought for any capacity and simple and inexpensive ones are now made for school theatres. One plate-dimmer can with skill be made to carry all dimming effects. For a group with initiative and a sense of adventure it is far more fun to make them. The simplest is a water resistance which requires only a length of drain tile, some cement and two pieces of copper. The method is to put a cement bottom into the flanged end of the tile, inserting a copper plate in the surface of the cement and leading a wire away from it through the cement and out at the base. The second piece of copper is fastened to another wire and the two wires are then hooked up with the circuit that feeds the lamp. The tile is filled with water and the free slug let down into it establishing a circuit. As the slug descends the light grows and is at its full intensity when the slug rests on the plate. A battery of six such dimmers can be made for five dollars. They should be rigged with small windlasses or some device which will permit them to be easily and smoothly operated. A switchboard for a school theatre is best made on a folding table.

For a Copeau stage the baby lens type of lamp is best. Several such lamps are clamped to upright pipe battens in the box pieces of the screen as shown in the drawing (Figure 4). Each lamp is assigned to one of the areas to be lighted for the action and is aimed in advance. Two dimmers should be used and one light faded slowly as the new one comes up. It is essential that the electrician should have a full view of the stage.

Dipping lamps in coloured lamp dye or collodion is rapidly becoming obsolete. A lamp of high enough wattage to be of any use will burn the colour off in an hour. Colour effects should be secured with a medium in front of the lamp housing. It can be of gelatine, of glassine paper tinted with dye, of glass or of silk.

Any dye dissolved in water with gum arabic or gum tragacanth will do to paint a glass or glassine medium, which should then be put in a double cardboard mask, secured with paper-fasteners and fixed in front of the lamp. After all, the regular gelatine media are best. They can be obtained in a wide range of colours from any theatre electrician. He either has them or he can get them. Coloured silk media are valuable for diffused light effects. If hard pushed the director can follow Inigo Jones and his generation of artists of the theatre. They put bottles of coloured water in front of their lamps.

VIII.   THE CHOICE OF THE PLAY

THE commonest difficulty of school groups is in the selection of the play.   Lack of discrimination at this juncture can go a long way towards wrecking promising effort.   The school theatre must, as I have said always be a supplement to the life of its community and, free as it is from most of the financial needs of the commercial theatre it can afford to do much better plays. In fact being worse off in acting talent it must always take care to be a little better off in play material.

The choice of plays should be governed by the director's pride in doing a fine thing, and his unwillingness to waste time and effort on an inferior thing.   If the director lacks this pride or if he lets it be overruled by the inevitable group of gratuitous advisers who love shoddy, his actors and technicians will soon regard him with contempt.   There is no test for trash in the theatre equal to that of having to memorize it and say it, or of having to listen to it over and over again in rehearsal.

A director who regards his work as a creative one will be careful to steer clear of certain mistakes.

He will not do plays that have been done in his town before unless he feels equal to the task of showing how they should have been done.

He will, unless there is some pressing reason, avoid revivals of his own successes.   They are always cold and dismal and although they may gratify the vanity of one or two actors they destroy the morale of the rest.   An artist wants to get on with something else.

He will give a wide berth to the current successes or even the recent successes in the commercial theatre. They are type actors' plays and require more virtuosity than he is likely to have in his company.

He will keep out of the well-worn and fatal grooves of the trade catalogue lists of plays for amateurs, for lodges, schools and churches. They are pitfalls for the undiscriminating.

If he wants quick access to good plays the director should possess himself first of a good collection, a few of which are listed below. The little theatre has now a fine literature of its own issued by the best publishers and it is easily available. An alert director can in a week find enough plays to last him for years. Frank Shay's "Thousand and One Plays for Little Theatres," is the most complete bibliography to date. It lists everything of distinction and gives the names of publishers. Both the British and American Drama Leagues have lists of plays, and most libraries have a special index of pieces suitable for little theatres. The director who plans to do sustained work should keep a note book in which he can enter play memoranda. He can easily enough remember all about a play but the trick is to be able to recall the plays he knows when he wants them.

No director of a school group can afford to forget the classics. Modernity in the theatre consists in the treatment of plays rather than in the plays themselves. A poor director can do yesterday's or today's play in so antiquated a manner that it does not deserve to get beyond rehearsal, and a good one can go back to the *Menæchmi* of Plautus or the *Phormio* of Terence and make it a jewel of modern comedy. He must remember that the modernity is his to make, not his to buy. He must remember also that the finest low comedy in extant literature still resides in Moliere's shorter pieces, in the Farce of Pierre Patelin, in Gammer Gurton's Needle, in the Danish folk plays of Ludwig Holberg, and most of all in the clown scenes from Shakespeare. For lighter comedy he must not forget Goldoni, Calderon, Marivaux, and de Musset, to mention only a few of them. I would not commend him as readily to the serious classics. They require more style than he will have at hand. All the way through except for an occasional thriller like the Dunsany plays he will do best to stay with the lighter side of life unless he has grown-ups in his casts. Young people lack the physical force to hold an audience through tragic scenes. They need the psychical release of a laugh.

Neither would I either in classical or modern plays recommend that they essay full time pieces. The short play is the natural medium of the little theatres, at least in their experimental years. Two one-act pieces make an excellent evening for a school theatre.

In the following bibliography I have leaned to the short play and mostly to the comedy, high, middle and low. I have given slight preference—not to the exclusion of others—to decorative plays. No director can afford to neglect the "making" end of the school theatre, if he is going to play for the public, and his craftsmen will be his greatest pride when all is done. Actors come and go. They happen more often than they are made. Craftsmen are made and they will make little theatres in their turn.

First in any list should come the collections of plays. They make play buying very inexpensive and will form the basis of a modest library of play material. Not all the plays in them are suitable for school use—that is too much to expect—but every one contains enough suitable pieces to be well worth its cost. I give below the title of each book and the name of its publisher. In the succeeding bibliography a play that occurs in one or more of the collections has the collection number or numbers in Roman numerals after it.

COLLECTIONS OF PLAYS

1. Atlantic Book of Modern Plays, edited by Sterling Andrus Leonard. Atlantic Monthly, Boston, 15 plays.

II. British Drama League Library of Plays. Brentano's, New York. Eight plays in four volumes.

III. Contemporary one-act plays, with outline studies and bibliographies, by B. Roland Lewis. Scribner, New York. 18 plays.

IV. Fifty Contemporary One-Act Plays. Edited by Frank Shay and Pierre Loving. Doubleday Page, New York. Fifty plays.

V. One-Act Plays by Modern Authors. Edited by Helen Louise Cohen. Harcourt Brace, New York. Sixteen plays.

VI. One-Act Plays. Edited by James Plaisted Webber and Hanson Hart Webster. Houghton Mifflin, Boston. Eighteen plays

VII. Representative One-Act Plays by American Authors. Selected with notes by Margaret G. Mayorga. Little Brown, Boston. Twenty-four plays.

VIII. Representative One-Act Plays by British and Irish Authors. Edited by Barrett H. Clark. Little Brown, Boston. Twenty plays.

IX. Representative One-Act Plays by Continental Authors, selected with biographical notes by Montrose J. Moses. Little Brown, Boston. Fifteen plays.

X. Short Plays by Representative Authors. Edited by Alice M. Smith. Macmillan, Toronto. Twelve plays.

XI. Ten Minute Plays. Edited by Pierre Loving. Brentano's, New York. Twelve plays.

XII. A Treasury of Plays for Children. Edited by Montrose J. Moses. Little Brown, Boston. Thirteen plays.

XIII. A Treasury of Plays for Men. Edited by Frank Shay. Little Brown, Boston, Twenty one plays.

XIV. A Treasury of Plays for Women. Edited by Frank Shay. Little Brown, Boston. Eighteen plays.

XV. Twenty Contemporary One-Act Plays. Edited by Frank Shay. Doubleday Page, New York. Twenty plays.

XVI. The World's Best Plays. Edited by Barret H. Clark. Samuel French, New York. This is really a series of thirty-five translations of foreign classics published separately at 25 cents each but it is so useful that although I have omitted other separate series from these collections I commend this to the attention of directors.

XVII. One-Act Plays of Today, compiled by J. W. Marriott, Harrap. London. Eleven plays.

XVIII. The Atlantic Book of Junior Plays. Atlantic Monthly, Boston. Thirteen plays.

XIX. Boccaccio's Untold Tale and nine other one-act plays, by Harry Kemp. Brentano's, New York. Ten plays.

XX. Mary The Third and other plays, by Rachel Crothers. Brentano's, New York. Three plays.

XXI. Expressing Willie and other plays, by Rachel Crothers Brentano's, New York. Three plays.

XXII. Four Plays For Four Women, by Alice Gerstenberg. Brentano's, New York. Four plays.

XXIII. Ten One-Act Plays, by Alice Gerstenberg. Brentano's, New York. Ten plays.

XXIV. Harvard Plays. Edited by Prof. Baker. Brentano's, New York. Twenty-four plays in six volumes.

XXV. One-Act Plays For Young Folks. Collated by Maurice Jagendorf. Brentano's, New York. Thirteen plays.

XXVI. Four One-Act Plays, by Lewis Beach. Brentano's New York. Four plays.

XXVII. Brentano's Contemporary Drama Series. containing the best of the season's dramatic offerings, one play in a volume. Brentano's, New York. Six plays.

XXVIII. The Plays of Bernard Shaw.
    "Heartbreak House" six plays,
    "Androcles and the Lion" three plays,
    "The Doctor's Dilemma" three plays,
    "John Bull's Other Island" three plays, two essays,
    "Misalliance" three plays,
    "Plays Pleasant and Unpleasant", seven plays,
    Brentano's, New York.

LIST OF PLAYS

In the following bibliography the Arabic numerals 1 to 28 refer to the list of publishers immediately following the play list. The same play will frequently be found in a volume with other pieces by the same author, issued separately by a second publisher and also, as indicated by the Roman figures, incorporated in a collection. Where a play is longer than a single act the fact is noted. The asterisks mark plays suited to younger children.

ANDREYEV, LEONID,—
> The Love of One's Neighbour. Satire. 15m. 7w. 3 children.
> IV.
> Samson in Chains. 9m. 4w. (4).
> He Who Gets Slapped. 7m. 4w. (4)
> Katerina 8m. 8w. (4)

ARISTOPHANES.—
> Lysistrata. Comedy. 4m. 5w. 1 child. XVI.

ARNOLD, JACK AND BURKE, EDWIN.—
> Good Medicine. Farce. 1m. 2w. (32)

AUGIER, EMILE.—
> The Postscript. Comedy. 1m. 2w. XVI.

BANNING, KENDALL AND KELLOCK, HAROLD.—
> Copy. Comedy. 7m. (32)

BARING, MAURICE.—
> The Aulis Difficulty. Comedy. 3m. 2w.
> The Blue Harlequin. Comedy. 3m. 1w.
> Catharine Parr. Comedy. 1m. 1w.
> The Drawback. Comedy. 1m. 1w.
> The Fatal Rubber. Comedy. 2m. 2w.
> The Greek Vase. Drama. 2m.
> Pious Æneas. Comedy. 2m. 1w.
> The Rehearsal. Comedy. 7m.
>> In 1 vol. *Diminutive Dramas.* (1)

BARKER H. GRANVILLE.—
  Rococo. Comedy. 3m. 3w. VIII.
  Vote By Ballot. Satire. 3m. 2w.
  Farewell to the Theatre. Comedy. 1m. 1w.
      In 1 vol. *Rococo and Other Plays.* (2)

BARRIE, SIR JAMES M. —
  Pantaloon. Comedy. 3m. 1w. 1 child.
  The Twelve Pound Look. Comedy. 2m. 2w. III.
  Rosalind. Comedy. 1m. 2w.
  The Will. Play. Three Scenes. 6m. 1w.
      In 1 vol. *Half Hours.* (3)
  The Old Lady Shows Her Medals. Play. 1m. 5w.
  The New Word. Play. 2m. 2w.
  Barbara's Wedding. Play. 3m. 1w.
  The Well Remembered Voice. Play. 2m. 2w.
      In 1 vol. *Echoes of the War.* (3)

BARRY, PHILIP.
  You and I. 4m. 3w. (4)

BEACH, LEWIS.—
  The Clod. Play. 4m. 1w. IV.
  A Guest for Dinner. Play. 4m.
  Love Among the Lions. Farce. 2m. 2w.
  Brothers. A Sardonic Comedy. 3m. IV.
      In 1 vol. *Four-One Act Plays.* (4)

BEITH, IAN HAY.—
  The Crimson Cocoanut. Comedy. 4m. 2w.
  A Late Delivery. Play. 3m. 2w.
  The Missing Card. Comedy. 2m. 2w.
      In 1 vol. *The Crimson Cocoanut and Other Plays.* (5)

BENAVENTE, JACINTO.—
  His Widow's Husband. Comedy. 2m. 5w. IV. (3)
  The Smile of the Mona Lisa. Play. 5m. 1 child. (6)

BENNETT, ARNOLD.—
  The Stepmother. Comedy. 2m. 2w. VIII.
  A Good Woman. Comedy. 2m. 1w. IV.
  A Question of Sex. Comedy. 2m. 2w.
      In 1 vol. *Polite Farces.* (7)

BERNARD, TRISTAN.—
   French without a Master. Comedy. 5m. 2w. XVI.
   I'm Going! Comedy.   1m. 1w. XVI.

BIRO, LAJOS.
   The Bridegroom. Play. 5m. 6w.
   The Grandmother. Play. 3m. 8w. IV.
      Drama Mag. May. 1918.

BRANCH, ANNA HEMPSTEAD.
   Rose o' the Wind. Play. 2m. 2w. (1)
   The Shoes that Danced. Play. 5m. 5w. VI. (1)

BRIEUX, EUGENE.
   A School for Mothers-in-Law. Comedy. 2m. 4w.
      Smart Set. Sept. 1913.

BRIGHOUSE, HAROLD.
   The Scaring Off of Teddy Dawson. Comedy. 2m. 2w. (8)
   Lonesome-Like. Play. 2m. 2w. I. VIII. (16)
   The Maid of France. Play. 3m. 2w. V. (16)
   Followers. Comedy 1m. 3w. VI.

BROWN, ALICE.
   The Hero. Play. 3m. 1w. Extras (men).
   Dr. Auntie. Comedy. 2m. 2w.
   The Crimson Lake. Play. 8m.
   Milly Dear. Play. 2m. 2w.
   The Web. "Cheap Melodrama." 3m. 2w.
   The Loving Cup. Rural Comedy. 4m. 9w.
   Joint Owners in Spain. Comedy. 4w.
   The Sugar House. Rural Play. 4m. 3w.
   A March Wind. Play. 2m. 2w. 1 child.
      In 1 vol. *One Act Plays.* (9)

BROWNING, ROBERT.
   In a Balcony. Poetic Drama. 1m. 2w.

de BRUEYS, DAVID AUGUSTIN. (*Collected Works.*)
   Pierre Patelin. Three Acts. Comedy. 7m. 2w. (8)

BUNNER, H. C.
   The Seven Old Ladies of Lavender Town. Operetta. 8m.
   8w. Music. XII.

BURNETT, FRANCIS HODGSON.
   *The Little Princess. Play. 3 Acts. 4m. 15w. Extras. XII.

CALDERON, GEORGE.
   The Little Stone House. Russian Tragedy. 5m. 2w. IV.
   Peace. Farce. 3m.
   Derelicts. Play. 3m. 3w. Extras.
   Gemini. Farce. 3m. 2w.
   Parkin Bros. Comedy. 3m.
   The Two Talismans. Comedy. 6m. Extras. 1w. Extras.
   The Lamp. Play. 2m. 1w. 1 child.
   Longing. "Subjective Drama." 10m. 2w. 1 child. Extras.
      In 1 vol. *Eight One-Act Plays.* (10)

CAMERON, MARGARET.
   Miss Doulton's Orchids. Comedy. 3m. 3w.
   The Burglar. Comedy. 5w.
   The Kleptomaniac. Comedy. 7w.
   The Pipe of Peace. Comedy. 1m. 2w.
   A Christmas Chime. Comedy. 2m. 2W.
   Committee on Matrimony. Comedy. 1m. 1w.
   Her Neighbour's Creed. Comedy. 1m. 1w.
      In 1 vol. *Comedies in Miniature.* (11)

CANNAN, GILBERT.
   Everybody's Husband. Comedy. 1m. 5w. (12)

CARMAN, BLISS AND KING, MARY.
   Earth Deities. Masque. 1m. 10w.
   The Dance Diurnal. Masque. 2m. 3w.
   Children of the Year. Masque. 1m. 1w. 24 children.
   Pas de Trois. Masque. 3m. 1w.
      In 1 vol. *Earth Deities and Other Masques.* (13)

CHAMBERS, C. HADDON.
   Open Gates. Play. 2m. 2w. (8)

CHATTERJI, TAPANMOHAN.
   The Light Bearer. Play. 4m. Drama Mag. Aug. 1918.

CHURCH, VIRGINIA.
   Pierrot by the Light of the Moon. Fantasy. 2m. 3w.
   Drama. Feb. 1919.

CLEMENTS, COLIN C.

Pierrot in Paris. Comedy. 2m. 2w.
Columbine. Comedy. 2w.
The Return of Harlequin. Comedy. 1m. 1w.
Three Lepers of Suk-el-Gareb. Play. 3m.
The Desert. Play. 3m. 6w.
The Siege. Play. 3w.
Moon Tide. Play. 2m.
In 1 vol. *Plays for a Folding Theatre.* (11)

CLEMENTS, COLIN C. AND SAUNDERS, JOHN M.

Love in a French Kitchen. Mediaeval Farce. 1m. 2w. (6)

CONRAD, JOSEPH.

One Day More. Play. 4m. 1w. Smart Set. Feb. 1914.

COPPÉE, FRANCOIS.

Pater Noster. Play. 3m. 3w. VI. XVI.

CROCKER, BOSWORTH.

The Last Straw. Play. 2m. 1w. 2 children. III.
The Baby Carriage. Play. 2m. 2w. IV.
The Dog. Play. 5m. 2w.
The First Time. Play. 3m. 2w.
The Cost of a Hat. Play. 2m. 2w.
In 1 vol. *Humble Folk.* (11)

CROTHERS, RACHEL

Expressing Willie. 6m. 5w. (4)
39 East. 9m. 5w. (4)
Nice People. 6m. 4w. (4)
Mary the Third. 5m. 8w. (4)
A Little Journey. 8m. 7w. (4)

CUMMINS, S. L.

*Blue Beard.
*Haroun-al-Raschid.
*St. George and the Dragon.
*The Sleeping Beauty.
*Torquil McFerron.
*Thomas Olihant and Tyranny.
In 3 vols. *Plays for Children.* (7)

DARGAN, OLIVE TILFORD AND PETERSON, F.
*The Flutter of the Gold Leaf.
*The Journey.
*Everychild.
*Two Doctors of Akragas.
 In 1 vol. *The Flutter of the Gold Leaf, etc.* (3)

DENISON, MERRILL.
Brothers in Arms. Comedy. 3m. 1w.
The Weather Breeder. Comedy. 4m. 1w.
From Their Own Place. Comedy. 5m. 1w.
 In 1 vol. *The Unheroic North.* (14)

DICKENS, CHARLES AND BROWN, H. P.
Twenty Dramatized Sketches, from the novels. (3)
Scenes from Dickens. James Edmund Jones. (14)

DIX, BEULAH MARIE.
Allison's Lad. 6m. VII.
The Hundreth Trick. Play. 4m.
The Weakest Link. Play. 4m.
The Snare and the Fowler. Play. 3m.
The Captain of the Gate. Play. 6m. I.
The Dark of the Dawn. Play. 4m.
 In 1 vol. *Allison's Lad and Other Poems.* (15)

DOWSON, ERNEST.
The Pierrot of the Minute. Fantasy. 1m. 1w. IV. V. (5)

DOWN, OLIPHANT.
The Maker of Dreams. Fantasy. 2m. 2w. V. VIII. (16

DOYLE, SIR ARTHUR CONAN.
Waterloo. Play. 3m. 2w. (8)
A Duet. Comedy. 1m. 1w. (8)

DRINKWATER, JOHN.
The God of Quiet. Allegory. 8m.
The Storm. Tragic Verse. 2m. 3w.
X=O. A Night of the Tojan War. Tragic Verse. 6m.
Cophetua. In verse. 8m. 1w. Extras.
 In 1 vol. *Pawns.* (1)

DUNSANY, LORD.
The Gods of the Mountain. Play. 10m.
The Golden Doom. Play. 10m. 2 children.

The Glittering Gate. Play. 2m.

King Argimenes and the Unknown Warrior. Play. 1m. 4w.

The Lost Silk Hat. Comedy. 5m.

   In 1 vol. *Five Plays.* (2)

A Night at an Inn. Play. 8m. V.

The Queen's Enemies. Play. 9m. 2w.

The Tents of the Arabs. Play. 5m. 1w.

The Laughter of the Gods. Three Acts. Play. 9m. 4w.

   In 1 vol. *Plays of Gods and Men.* (17)

Fame and The Poet. Satire. 2m. 1w. I.

ECHEGARAY, JOSE.

   The Street Singer. Play. 2m. 2w. Drama Mag. Feb. 1917.

EDGERTON, LADY ALIX.

   Masque of the Two Strangers. 14 characters. (18) V.

EMERY, GILBERT.

   Thank You, Doctor. Melodramatic Farce. 3m. 2w. (32)

FERGUSON, J. A.

   Campbell of Kilmhor. Play. 4m. 2w. 1. (16)

FEUILLET, OCTAVE.

   The Fairy. Comedy. 3m. 1w. XVI.

   The Village. Comedy. 2m. 2w. XVI.

FITZMAURICE, GEORGE.

   The Magic Glasses. Play. 3m. 2w.

   The Pie Dish. Play. 4m. 2w. 3 children.

   The Dandy Dolls. Play. 4m. 2w. 3 children.

      With two long plays in 1 vol. (2)

FRANCE, ANATOLE.

   The Man Who Married a Dumb Wife. Two Acts. Comedy. 14m. 4w. (19)

GALSWORTHY, JOHN.

   The First and the Last. Play. 2m. 1w.

   The Little Man. Three scenes. Comedy. 9m. 2w. V.

   Hall Marked. "A Satiric Trifle." 4m. 4w. 2 dogs.

   Defeat. A Tiny Drama. 1m. 1w.

   The Sun. Comedy. 1m. 1w. I.

   Punch and Go. Comedy. 8m. 2w.

      In 1 vol. *Six Short Plays.* (3)

GERSTENBERG, ALICE.
 Alice in Wonderland. 3 acts. 13m. 4w. XII.

GIACOSA, GIUSEPPE.
 The Wager. Comedy. 4m. 1w. XVI.

GILBERT, W. S.
 Sweethearts. Two acts. Comedy. 2m. 2w. (8)
 Rosencrantz and Guildenstern. Comedy. 5m. 2w. (8)
 Comedy and Tragedy. Play. 14m. 2w. (8)

GLASPELL, SUSAN.
 Trifles. Tragedy. 3m. 2w. IV.
 The People. Play. 10m. 2w.
 Close the Book. Satirical Comedy. 3m. 5w.
 The Outside. Play. 3m. 2w.
 A Woman's Honour. Play. 2m. 6w. 2 Extras.
  In 1 vol. *Plays.* (20).

GOODMAN, KENNETH SAWYER.
 Back of the Yards. Play. 3m. 2w.
 Dust of the Road. Play. 4m. 4w.
 Ephraim and the Winged Bear. Comedy. 4m. 3w.
 A Game of Chess. Play. 4m.
 Barbara. Play. 2m. 1w.
 The Dancing Dolls. Play. 4m. 7w.
 A Man Can Only Do His Best. Comedy. 6m. 2w.
  Published separately. (21)

GOODMAN, K.S. AND STEVENS, THOMAS WOOD.
 Holbein in Blackfriars. Comedy. 6m. 2w.
 Ryland. Comedy. 5m. 2w. VII.
 Reinald and the Red Wolf. Masque. 19m. 6w. and extras.
 Caesar's Gods. Masque. 12m. 3w. and extras.
 The Masque of Quitzal's Bowl. 7m.
 The Daimio's Head, Masque. 13m. 5w.
 The Masque of Montezuma. 16m. 4w. and extras.
  Published separately (21)

GREGORY, LADY.
 Spreading the News. Comedy. 7m. 3w. I. V. VIII. X.
 The Rising of the Moon. Comedy. 4m. VI.
 The Jackdaw. Comedy. 4m. 2w.
 The Workhouse Ward. Comedy. 2m. 1w. IV.

The Travelling Man. Play. 1m. 1w. 1 child.
The Gaol Gate. Play. 1m. 2w.
Hyacinth Halvey. Comedy. 3m. 3w. III.
    In 1 vol. *Plays*. (17)
The Bogie Man. Comedy. 2m.
The Full Moon. Comedy. 5m. 3w.
Coats. Comedy. 4m. 1w.
Damer's Gold. Comedy. 4m. 1w.
McDonough's Wife. Comedy. 1m. 2w.
    In 1 vol. (26)

HAMILTON, COSMO.
St. Martin's Summer. Comedy. 1m. 2w.
Soldiers' Daughters. Comedy. 3w.
Toller's Wife. Comedy. 4m. 1w.
Why Cupid Came to Earl's Court. Comedy. 3m. 4w.
    In 1 vol. *Short Plays for Small Stages*. (22)

HOPKINS, ARTHUR
Moonshine. Play. 2m. III. (8)

HOUGHTON, STANLEY.
The Dear Departed. Comedy. 3m. 3w.
Fancy Free. Comedy. 2m. 2w. VIII.
The Master of the House. Play. 4m. 2w.
Phipps. Comedy. 2m. 1w.
The Fifth Commandment. Play. 2m. 2w.
    In 1 vol. *Five Plays*. (8)

HOUSMAN, LAURENCE.
The Queen, God Bless Her! 3m. 1w.
His Favorite Flower. 2m. 1w.
The Comforter. 3m. 2w.
Possessions. 2m. 5w.
    In 1 vol. *Angels and Ministers*. (23)
The Christmas Tree. 1m. 1w. 1 child.
The Torch of Time. 4m.
Moonshine. 4m.
A Fool and His Money. 3m.
The House Fairy. 2w. 1 child.
    In 1 vol. *False Premises*. Vol. 1 of II.
Good as Gold. Morality play. 7m. (8)

Bird in Hand. 10m. 3w. (8)

A Likely Story. Comedy. 4m. 1w. (8)

The Lord of the Harvest. Play. 6m. 1w. (8)

Nazareth. Play. 13m. 3w. (8)

The Snow Man. Play. 3m. 2w. VIII. (8)

The Return of Alcestis. Play. 15m. 20w. (8)

HUDSON, HOLLAND.

The Shepherd in the Distance. Fantasy. 4m. 5w. and extras. IV. (11)

The Pearl of Dawn. Fantasy in 10 Scenes. 7m. 3w. extras. Action! XVII. XV.

IRVING, LAURENCE.

The Phoenix. Play. 2m. 2w. (8)

IZUMO, TAKEDA.

Matsuo, the Pine Tree. 5m. 3w. 3 children and extras.

JACOBS, W. W. with various others.

A Love Passage. Comedy. 3m. 1w.

The Ghost of Jerry Bundler. Play. 7m.

Admiral Peters. Comedy. 2m. 1w.

The Monkey's Paw. Play. 4m. 1w.

The Changeling. Comedy 2m. 1w.

The Boatswain's Mate. Play. 2m. 1w.

In the Library. Comedy. 5m.

Published separately. (8)

KARINTHY, FREDERICK.

The Drama. Farce. 4m. (32)

KELLY, GEORGE.

Finders Keepers. Play. 1m. 2w. XV. (11)

KNOBLOCK, EDWARD.

My Lady's Grace. Comedy. 1m. 3w. VI.

LEACOCK, STEPHEN AND HASTINGS, BASIL.

"Q". Farce. (8)

LESAGE, ALAIN RENÉ.

Crispin, His Master's Rival. Comedy. 4m. 3w. XVI.

LUTKENHAUS, A. A.

*Master Skylark. 11m. 3w. extras. XII.

MACKAY, CONSTANCE D'ARCY.
 *The Silver Thread. 3 acts. 14m. 5w. and extras. XII.
 *The Forest Spring. Comedy. 1m. 3w.
 *The Foam Maiden. Comedy. 1m. 2w.
 *Troll Magic. Comedy. 11 char. and extras.
 *The Three Wishes. Comedy. 2m. 1w.
 *Siegfried. Play. 3m. 1w.
 *A Brewing of Brains. Comedy. 1m. 2w.
 *The Snow Witch. Comedy. 2m. 4w. and extras.
  In 1 vol. *The Silver Thread, etc.* (15)

MACMILLAN, MARY.
 The Shadowed Star. Play. 3m. 5w. IV. X.
 The Ring. Comedy. 7m. 3w.
 The Rose. Comedy. 1m. 2w.
 Luck? Comedy. 6m. 7w.
 Entr'Acte. Play. 1m. 2w.
 A Woman's a Woman for a' That. Comedy. 2m. 3w.
 A Fan and Two Candlesticks. Play. 2m. 1w.
 A Modern Masque. Play. 3m. 1w.
 The Futurists. Play. 8w.
 The Cate of Wishes. Play. 1m. 1w. 1 child.
  In 1 vol. *Short Plays.* (11)
 His Second Girl. Play. 3m. 3w.
 At the Church Door. Play. 2m. 2w.
 Honey. 3 acts. Comedy. 2m. 3w. 1 child.
 The Dress Rehearsal of Hamlet. Comedy. 10 w.
 The Pioneers. Play. 10m. 3w. 5 children.
 In Mendelesia I. Play. 5w.
 In Mendelesia II. Play. 5w.
 The Dryad. Play. 1m. 2w.
  In 1 vol. *More Short Plays.* (11)
 The Week End. Play. 3 acts. 1m. 2w.
 The Storm. Play. 1m. 11w.
 In Heaven. Play. 4m.
 When Two's Not Company. Comedy. 2m.
 Peter Donelly. Play. 1m. 3w.
 An Apocryphal Episode. Comedy. 2m. 2w.
 Standing Moving. Comedy. 2m. 2w.
  In 1 vol. *Third Book of Short Plays.* (11)

MAETERLINCK, MAURICE.
>   Interior. Play. 4m. 3w. 2 children. (16)
>   A Miracle of St. Anthony. 15 characters. (25)

MARIVAUX, PIERRE.
>   The Legacy. Comedy. 4m. 2w. XVI.

MARKS, JEANNETTE.
>   The Merry Merry Cuckoo. Play. 3m. 2w. VII. X.
>   The Welsh Honeymoon. Play. 3m. 2w. V.
>   The Deacon's Hat. Comedy. 3m. 3w. III.
>   In 1 vol. *Three Welsh Plays*. (2)

MASEFIELD, JOHN.
>   The Locked Chest. Play. 4m. 1w. X.
>   The Sweeps of Ninety-Eight. Comedy. 5m. 1w.
>   In 1 vol. (9)
>   Good Friday. Passion Play. 7m. 1w. (9)

MAUREY, MAX.
>   Rosalie. Comedy. 1m. 2w. XVI.

MEILHAC AND HALEVY.
>   Panurge's Sheep. Comedy. 1m. 2w. XVII.
>   Indian Summer. Comedy. 2m. 2w. XVI.

MERINGTON, MARGUERITE.
>   The Testing of Sir Gawayne. 6m. 4w. Extras. XII.

MILLAY, EDNA ST. VINCENT.
>   Ario da Capo. A Play in Blank Verse. 4m. 1w. IV. (13)
>   Two Slatterns and a King. 2m. 2w. XV. (11)
>   The Lamp and the Bell. Historical verse. 5 Acts. 13m.
>   21w. 8 children. XIV.

MILNE. A. A.
>   Wurzel Flummery. Comedy. 3m. 2w. V.
>   The Boy Comes Home. Comedy. 2m. 2w. VI.

de MILLE, W. C. AND BARNARD, CHARLES.
>   The Forest Ring. 3 acts. 2m. 2w. 5 fairies. 4 animals.
>   XII.

MOLIERE, JEAN BAPTISTE POQUELIN.
>   The Doctor in Spite of Himself. Comedy. 3 Acts. 8m. 3w.
>   The Miser. Comedy. 5 acts. 9m. 4w.
>   The Rogueries of Scapin. Comedy. 3 acts. 9m. 3w.

In 1 vol. *The Kiltartan Moliere*. Translated into Irish dialect by Lady Gregory. (26)

The Doctor in Spite of Himself. Comedy. 3 Acts. 8m. 3w. XVI.

The Sicilian. Two acts. Comedy. 4m. 3w. XVI.

The Affected Young Ladies. Comedy. 6m. 3w. XVI.

MORRISON, ARTHUR.

That Brute Simmons. Comedy. 2m. 1w. (8)

MUKERJI, DHAN GOPAL.

The Judgment of Indra. Drama. 4m. 1w. XIII.

deMUSSET, ALFRED.

Barberine. Three Act Comedy. 5m. 2w.

Fantasio. Two Act Comedy. 8m. 2w.

No Trifling with Love. Three Act Comedy. 4m. 3w.

A Door Must Be Open or Shut. Comedy. 2m.

A Caprice. Comedy. 1m. 2w.

One Cannot Think of Everything. Comedy. 3m. 2w.

In 1 vol. *Barberine and Other Comedies*. (27)

deMUSSET, ALFRED AND AUGIER, EMILE.

The Green Coat. Comedy. 3m. 1w. XVI.

O'NEILL, EUGENE.

Thirst. Play. 2m. 1w.

The Web. Play. 5m. 1w.

Warnings. Play. 5m. 4w.

Fog. Play. 3m. 1w.

Recklessness. Play. 3m.

In 1 vol. *Thirst and Other One-Act Plays*. (6)

The Moon of the Caribbees. Play. 17m. 4w.

Bound East for Cardiff. Play. 11m.

The Long Voyage Home. Play. 8m. 3w.

In the Zone. Play. 9m. VII.

Ile. Play. 5m. 1w. I. IV.

Where the Cross is Made. Play. 6m. 1w.

The Rope. Play. 3m. 2w.

In 1 vol. *The Moon of the Caribbees*. (25)

PINERO, SIR ARTHUR WING.

Playgoers. Comedy. 2m. 6w. (8)

Hester's Mystery. Comedy. 3m. 2w. (8)

The Money Spinner. Two act play. 5m. 3w. (8)

PLAUTUS.
  The Twins. Comedy. 7m. 2w. XVI.
POLLOCK, CHANNING.
  The Fool. 13m. 7w. (4)
QUINTERO, SERAFIN AND JOAQUIN ALVAREZ.
  A Sunny Morning. Comedy. 2m. 2w. IV. VI.
ROBERTSON, W. GRAHAM.
  Pinkie and the Fairies. 1m. 3w. 5 fairies. 8 characters.
    Extras. XII.
  Punch and Judy. Puppet Show. XII.
ROSSETTI, CHRISTINA G.
  The Months, A pageant. 6m. 6w. Extras. XII.
ROSTAND, EDMOND.
  The Romancers. Three Act Comedy. 5m. 1w. and extras. VI.
SARDOU, VICTORIEN.
  The Black Pearl. Comedy. 7m. 3w. XVI.
SARG, TONY AND WILLIAMSON, HAMILTON.
  *The Three Wishes. XII.
SHAW, GEORGE BERNARD.
  How He Lied to Her Husband. Comedy. 2m. 1w. (4)
  The Dark Lady of the Sonnets. Comedy. 2m. 2w. (4)
  Overruled. Comedy. 2m. 2w. (4)
  Great Catherine. Farce. 4 scenes. 4m. 4w. (4)
SMITH, NORA ARCHIBALD.
  *In the Good Old Days. Comedy. 4m. 3w.
  *The Quest of the Doll. Comedy. 2m. 4w. and extras.
  *The Wonderful Tea-Kettle. 3 Act Comedy. 7 characters.
  *Hilltop and Hillfoot. Comedy. 3m. 2w. 1 child.
  *The Crowning of Peace. Masque. 2m. 3w.
  *Goldilocks and the Three Bears. 2m. 1w. 1 child.
  *Red Riding Hood. Comedy. 2m. 3w. 1 wolf.
  *The Elves and the Shoemaker. Pantomime. 7 characters.
      In 1 vol. Plays. Pantomimes and Tableaux. (30)
SOPHOCLES.
  Antigone. Arranged for schools. 11 characters. (5)
STEVENS, WALLACE.
  Three Travellers Watch a Sunrise. 5m. 1w. IV.
STRONG, AUSTIN.
  *The Toymaker of Nuremberg. 3 acts. 14m. 2w. Extras. XII.

SUTRO, ALFRED.
    The Man in the Stalls. Comedy. 2m. 1w.
    A Marriage Has Been Arranged. Comedy. 1m., 1w.
    The Man on the Kerb. Comedy. 1m. 1w. X.
    The Open Door. Comedy. 1m. 1w.
    The Bracelet. Comedy. 5m. 3w.
        In 1 vol. *Five Little Plays.* (4)

SYNGE, JOHN MILLINGTON.
    The Shadow of the Glen. Play. 3m. 1w. V. (17)
    Riders to the Sea. Play. 3m. 5w. and extras. I.
    VIII. (17)
    The Tinker's Wedding. Play. 1m. 2w. (17)

TAGORE, RABINDRANATH.
    Sangasi. 17m. 7w.
    Malini. 2 Acts. 8m. 2w. 1 boy. Extras.
    Sacrifice. 2 Acts. 8m. 2w. Extras.
    The King and the Queen. 13m. 4w. Extras.
        In 1 vol. *Sacrifice and Other Plays.* (9)
    Chitra. Play. 3m. 1w. (9)
    The King of the Dark Chamber. 27m. 3w. Extras. (9)
    The Post Office. Play. 9m. 1w. 1 child and extras. (9)

TARKINGTON, BOOTH.
    Beauty and the Jacobin. Comedy. 3m. 2w. (28)
    The Ghost Story. Comedy. 5m. 5w. (11)
    The Trysting Place. Comedy. 4m. 3w. (11)

TCHEKHOFF, ANTON.
    On the High Road. Play. 8m. 3w.
    The Proposal. Comedy. 2m. 1w.
    The Wedding. Farce. 7m. 3w.
    The Boor. Farce. 2m. 1w. III. IV.
    A Tragedian in Spite of Himself. Farce. 2m.
    Anniversary. Farce. 2m. 2w.
        In 1 vol. *Plays. Second Series.* (3)
    The Swan Song. Comedy. 2m. X.
        With longer plays in *Plays. First Series.* (3)

TENNYSON, ALFRED LORD.
    The Falcon. Poetic drama. 2m. 2w.
        In *Collected Works.*

TERENCE.

Phormio. Comedy. 11m. 2w. XVI.

THEURIET, ANDRE.

Jean Marie. Play. 2m. 1w. XVI.

WALKER, STUART.

*The Trimplet. Comedy. 2m. 2w.
*Nevertheless. Comedy. 1m. 1 boy. 1 girl. VI.
*Six Who Pass While the Lentils Boil. Comedy. 5m. 3w.
4 extras. VII. X. XII.
*The Medicine Show. Comedy. 3m. IV.
    In 1 vol. *Portmanteau Plays.* (11)
The Lady of the Weeping Willow Tree. 3 acts. 2m. 4w.
The Very Naked Boy. Comedy. 1m. 1w. 1 boy.
Jonathan Makes a Wish. 3 acts. Fantasy. 6m. 2w.
2 children.
    In 1 vol. *More Portmanteau Plays.* (11)
Gammer Gurton's Needle. 6m. 5w.
The Birthday of the Infanta. 2m. 1w. 8 children.
Sir David Wears a Crown. Fantasy. 14m. 4w. XV.
    In 1 vol. *Portmanteau Adaptations.* (11)

WYATT, EUPHEMIA VAN RENSSELAER.

Her Country. Tragedy. 2m. 1w. (32)

YEATS, WILLIAM BUTLER.

The Countess Cathleen. Play. 3 Acts. 6m. 3w. Extras.
The Land of Heart's Desire. Fantasy. Verse. 3m. 3w.
The Shadowy Waters. Fantasy. 5m. 1w. Extras.
The King's Threshold. Fantasy. 11m. 5w. Extras.
On Bailie's Strand. Poetic Fantasy. 5m. Extras. 8m.
3 singing w.
Deirdre. Tragedy. 5m. 4w.
    In 1 vol. Dramatic Works. (9)
The Hour Glass. Fantasy. 3m. 1w. 2 children. Extra
children.
Cathleen Ni Houlihan. Play. 3m. 3w.
A Pot of Broth. Comedy. 2m. 1w.
    In 1 vol. (9)
The Green Helmet. An Heroic Farce. 5m. 3w. Extras. (9)

BOOKS ON PLAY PRODUCING

CLARK, BARRETT H.   How to produce Amateur Plays. (2)

BEEGLE-CRAWFORD.   Community Drama and Pageantry
Yale University Press, New Haven.

MACKAY, CONSTANCE D'ARCY.   Costumes and Scenery
for Amateurs. (15)

TAYLOR, EMERSON.   Practical Stage Directing for
Amateurs. (29)

MITCHELL, ROY. Shakespeare for Community Players. (30)

PRICE, WILLIAM T. The Technique of the Drama. (4)

LIST OF PUBLISHERS

(1)   Houghton Mifflin Co., 4 Park Street, Boston, Mass.

(2)   Little, Brown & Co., 34 Beacon Street, Boston, Mass.

(3)   Charles Scribner's Sons, 597 Fifth Avenue, New York City.

(4)   Brentano's, Fifth Avenue and 27th Street, New York, City.

(5)   Walter H. Baker Co., 5 Hamilton Place, Boston, Mass.

(6)   Richard Badger, 194-200 Boylston Street, Boston, Mass.

(7)   George H. Doran Co., 244 Madison Avenue, New York City.

(8)   Samuel French, 21 West 38th Street, New York City.

(9)   The Macmillan Company of Canada, 70 Bond Street, Toronto.

(10)   Grant Richards, 8 St. Martins Street, Leicester Square, W.C.2,
London, England.

(11)   D. Appleton & Co., 29-35 West 32nd Street, New York City.

(12)   B. W. Huebsch, 116 West 13th Street, New York City.

(13)   Mitchell Kennerley, Park Avenue and 59th Street, New York
City.

(14)   McClelland & Stewart, 215 Victoria Street, Toronto, Ont.

(15)   Henry Holt & Co., 19 West 44th Street, New York City.

(16)   LeRoy Phillips, 41 Winter Street, Boston, Mass.

(17)   John W. Luce & Co., 212 Summer Street, Boston ,Mass.

(18)   Gowans & Gray, 5 Robert Street, Adelphi, W.C.2, London,
England.

(19)   Dodd, Mead & Co., Fourth Avenue and 30th Street, New
York City.

(20)   Small, Maynard & Co., 41 Mt. Vernon Street, Boston, Mass.

(21)   Stage Guild, Railway Exchange Building, Chicago, Ill.

(22)   Skeffington & Son, 34 Paternoster Row, E.C.4, London,
England.

(23)   Harcourt, Brace, 1 West 47th Street, New York City.

(24)   Duffield & Co., 211 East 19th Street, New York City.

(25)   Boni & Liveright, 105 West 49th Street, New York City.

(26)   Putnam Sons, 2 West 45th Street, New York City.

(27)   Charles H. Sergel Co., 542 S. Dearborn Street, Chicago, Ill.

(28)   Harper & Sons, 324 Pearl Street, New York City.

(29)   J. M. Dent & Sons, 215 Victoria Street, Toronto, Ont.

(30)   Moffat, Yard & Co., 30 Union Square, New York City.

(31)   Thomas Y. Crowell, 426 West Broadway, New York City.

(32)   Longmans, Green & Co., 210 Victoria Street, Toronto, Ont.

SHOPPING LIST

Non-professional groups experience great difficulty in getting some of the materials used in the theatre. Often the thing required is never seen in the shops but is supplied direct to some trade or other and while in common use is hard to find. The following list is by no means complete either as to materials or to dealers but it gives at least one address at which each of the commonest needs may be supplied. In most cases the inquirer will find some other nearer at home.

DRY COLOUR, ANILINE, BRONZE POWDER, STAIN, ETC.
  The E. Harris Company, 73 King Street, East, Toronto.
  James W. Paton, 20 Temperance Street.
  Easter Color and Chem. Co., 145 Nassau Street, N.Y. City.

BURLAPS AND SACKINGS.
  Fulton Bag & Cotton Mills, Inc., 330 Wythe Ave., Brooklyn.
  The Canadian Bag Co., 100 Paton Road, Toronto.

STAGE HARDWARE, RIGGING, BRACES, ETC.
  Peter Clark, Inc., 534 W. 30th Street, New York City.
  Charles Gallagher, 34 Edgewood Avenue, Toronto.

LAMPS, GELATINE MEDIA, AND FITTINGS.
  Kliegel Bros., 321 West 50th Street, New York City.
  A. E. Jackson, 54 Alberta Street, Toronto.

TIGHTS, FLESHINGS, STAGE COSTUME FABRICS.
  Morris I. Kohan, 290 Taaffe Place, Brooklyn, N.Y.
  J. J. Wylie & Co., 18-20 East 27th Street, New York City.

PLAY BOOKS AND BOOKS ABOUT THE THEATRE.
  If the dealer in the director's town or city is unable to get the item needed, there are three firms that make a specialty of play finding. They can also advise about royalties. They are:

  The Poetry Bookshop, 35 Devonshire Street, London, W.C., England.

  The Gotham Book Mart, West 45th Street, New York City.
  Brentano's, 225 Fifth Avenue, New York City.

  For complete lists of theatrical equipment and material:
  The Theatrical Business Men's Guide, published by H. P. Hanaford, 1400 Broadway, New York City ($.25 per copy).